GOLD FLEET FOR CALIFORNIA

Oh! Californy!
That's the land for me!
I'm bound for Sacramento
With the washbowl on my knee.

—Song of 1849.

In
memory of
Coy
who so much wanted
to see this book
published

Also by Charles Bateson
THE CONVICT SHIPS 1787–1868

GOLD FLEET
FOR CALIFORNIA

rty-Niners from Australia and New Zealand

by Charles Bateson

MICHIGAN STATE UNIVERSITY PRESS
EAST LANSING

Copyright 1963 by Charles Bateson
First published in the United States of America in 1964 by
The Michigan State University Press
Library of Congress Catalog Card Number: 64–11360
Designed by Sally Keep
Printed in Australia by Waite & Bull Pty. Limited,
Strawberry Hills, Sydney

★
  ★
★
   ★
★

CONTENTS

MY THANKS go to many people for assisting in the gathering of the material for this book, which could not have been written without their enthusiastic co-operation. If I have inadvertently omitted the name of any individual in this acknowledgment, I can only say his or her help was nevertheless appreciated.

Agnes C. Conrad, Archivist, Territory of Hawaii, answered questions in her official capacity and gave generously of her own time to check many facts. To her I owe the data of arrival and departure dates for Hawaii. Mr. Barr Thompkins, of the Bancroft Library, University of California, and Mrs. Hester Robinson, of the Society of California Pioneers, San Francisco, were equally generous in providing similar information for San Francisco. Mr. Karl Kortum, director of the San Francisco Maritime Museum, placed me in touch with Mr. Thompkins and Mrs. Robinson and provided other information.

Mr. R. Duthie, City Librarian, Auckland Public Libraries, and the staff of the Central Library, Auckland, compiled lists of sailings for, and of arrivals from, California for New Zealand and went to much trouble to verify information. Mr. A. C. W. Dunningham, City Librarian, Dunedin Public Library, Mr. J. O. Wilson, Chief Librarian, General Assembly Library, Parliament House, Wellington, the Librarian, Alexander Turnbull Library, Wellington, the Comptroller of Customs, Wellington, and Mr. G. L. O'Halloran, Secretary of the Marine Department, Wellington, also helped with the New Zealand section.

The trustees of the Mitchell Library, Sydney, granted permission to quote from manuscripts in their unrivalled collection of Australiana, and I have made free use of this permission with the Towns Correspondence, the Colonial Secretary's Papers, the Shipping Reports, the Hobler Journal and other manuscript material in the

7

library. The librarian and staff facilitated my examination of these sources, and their courtesy and readiness to help on all occasions is a pleasurable memory of long hours spent in the library. Similar assistance came from the staffs of the Public Library of New South Wales, of the State Library of Tasmania, in particular Mr. Robert Sharman (who is now in Brisbane), Mr. Peter Eldershaw and the staff of the Archives section, and of the Public Library of South Australia, especially Mr. J. McLellan, Archivist. Dr. Morris Watt, of Dunedin, helped with many particulars of New Zealand vessels.

My special thanks are due to Mr. F. A. Meere, former Comptroller-General of Customs and Excise, Canberra, for permission to examine the ship registers in the custody of his department, and to successive Registrars of British Ships at the Sydney Customs House, especially Mr. F. Wright, Mr. J. Portlock and Mr. L. Wyche, for their co-operation in making the registers available for my inspection.

Mrs. F. G. Marginson, of Hamilton, Brisbane, obtained for me from the late Miss Dorothy Rowsell, Capt. Fox's grand-daughter, the unique illustration of the *Phantom*, the *Emma* and the *Chearful* off Port Jackson, and the portraits of Captain Henry Thomas Fox, master of the *Mary Catherine*, and of his wife, Isobel. Mrs. Marginson also furnished copies of Captain Fox's private log of his passage to San Francisco and of his letters describing the *Mary Catherine's* voyage, and drew my attention to the captain's account of his return passage which was published in the *Sydney Morning Herald* of 17th December 1851, and in the *Nautical Magazine* of May 1856. Mr. George McCadden, of New York, gave invaluable assistance in obtaining illustrations from American sources.

My wife and daughter constantly encouraged me, rendering much practical help and making many suggestions.

Readers who may be able to correct errors in the text or who are able to supply additional information are asked to write me at Box 4922, G.P.O., Sydney, N.S.W., Australia. I shall welcome all correspondence tending to throw light upon Australia's maritime history.

CHARLES BATESON,
Sydney

1 *MIGRATION IN MASS*

ON 24th JANUARY 1848, when San Francisco was a slumbering settlement of less than a thousand souls and not more than fifteen thousand people were scattered through the whole of California, young James Wilson Marshall found gold in the tail race of Sutter's Mill, standing on the banks of the Sacramento River near the site of what is now Coloma.

This chance happening caused the greatest mass migration since the Crusades, drawing over a quarter of a million people to the new American state of California within two years.

Among them were several thousand people from Australia and New Zealand. These two recently founded British colonies, the former little more than sixty, the latter barely forty, years old, were themselves sparsely populated. Yet with the announcement of the discovery of gold in California, Australians and New Zealanders began crossing the Pacific to San Francisco, and their numbers increased as the months went by. Sailing vessels of every description, from large ocean-going ships, barques and brigs to small coastal cutters, brigantines and schooners, were dispatched to California, every inch of available space aboard occupied by gold-seekers or goods.

That so many Australians should have sailed for California was ironic for, though none knew it at the time, the great island continent of the south was itself rich in gold. Three years after Marshall's discovery an Australian digger, Edward Hammond Hargraves, returned to New South Wales from California to wash the first pan of gold-bearing gravel at Ophir. Within a few months the tide of migration had been reversed and thousands upon thousands of gold-seekers were flocking into Australia.

The presence of gold in California had been detected by Sir Francis Drake's expedition in 1579, when he had careened the *Golden Hind* in a small bay to the northward of San Francisco Bay. One hundred and forty-two years later, in 1721, the privateer George Shelvocke, on his semi-piratical excursion into the Pacific, had noted that the soil was richly auriferous. But no attempt to develop California's mineral wealth followed the visits of either Drake or Shelvocke.

James Wilson Marshall was a New Jersey wagon-builder who had become boss carpenter at Sutter's Mill. If the fact of his discovery is well authenticated, the details are shrouded in myth and legend. However, they are unimportant. It is immaterial whether Marshall found on that January day a few flakes of gold dust or a piece of metal half the size of a pear. Nor does it matter whether he realized he had discovered gold or thought he had picked up some iron pyrites.

Whatever his find, it at first aroused little interest. Marshall's claims were ridiculed when he took his samples to be tested. His employer, Captain John Augustus Sutter, was incredulous and unenthusiastic. This handsome German-Swiss ex-army officer had arrived in California in 1839 with a party of twelve men and three women and had obtained a fifty-thousand-acre land grant by swearing allegiance to the Mexican flag.

Ten years later, from a picturesque timber and adobe castle whose ramparts mounted a dozen cannon, Sutter ruled over some hundreds of Indians and a number of American immigrants who rented small farms from him. His workshops produced blankets, shirts and hats; his tanneries turned out leather of excellent quality; he traded tallow, wheat, flour, hides, fur and other articles. His interests were widespread and varied, his trade was extensive. He was the most successful and powerful man in the Sacramento valley. His sole worry concerned his land grants. He was convinced California would fall to the United States and he feared his grants might not be confirmed.

When Marshall finally convinced his employer he had found gold, Sutter did the most natural thing in the world: he tried desperately to suppress news of the discovery. The attempt was futile. Sutter's secrecy delayed but did not stop the influx of miners. Gradually word leaked out. A few hundred miners, arriving singly and in small parties over a period of several weeks, were soon at work. Sutter doubled the wages of his workmen in a vain effort to prevent them from rushing off to join the ranks of the gold-seekers.

Then, in April 1848, astute Sam Brannan, who had reached San Francisco in 1846 as leader of a shipload of Mormons and who owned a well-stocked store at Sutter's Fort, came up river. On his return to San Francisco, Brannan ran up and down Montgomery Street waving a bottle and shouting: 'Gold! Gold! This bottle is full of gold dust! There are placeros in the Sierras that are the richest in the world! Hurrah for California!' He then brought out an extra edition of his newspaper and dispatched copies by Indian couriers far and wide.

The rush now began in earnest. San Francisco, Monterey, San Jose, Santa Cruz—every settlement and hamlet—were deserted by all but a handful of their inhabitants. By early June more than two thousand diggers were camped in the immediate vicinity of Sutter's Fort, and their numbers were swelled every day by new arrivals. Businesses of every kind closed their doors, farms were left untilled, stock untended. Employers and employees, the proprietors of businesses and the owners of farms as well as their clerks, mechanics, workmen and labourers, shouldered their packs and set forth to make quick fortunes.

As Walter Colton, alcalde of Monterey, wrote : 'The blacksmith dropped his hammer, the carpenter his plane, the mason his trowel, the farmer his sickle, the baker his loaf, and the tapster his bottle. All were off for the mines, some on horses, some on carts and some on crutches, and one went in a litter.'[1]

Beyond California, the news necessarily travelled slowly and irrationally. Wireless and the aeroplane had yet to be invented. Telegraphy was still in the experimental stage; a submarine cable was not to be laid under the English Channel from Dover to Brest until 1850, and not until seven years later was the first attempt to lay one under the Atlantic to end in failure. No railway linked the eastern and western coasts of the vast American continent.

To carry the news there were only the sailing ship, graceful under her towering spread of canvas, but with her speed depending upon the vagaries of wind and sea, and the early steamship, whose primitive engines and insatiable demand for fuel rendered her unreliable. So China received the news before New York; London heard but a short time before the remote lands of Australia and New Zealand.

When eventually word of Marshall's discovery spread round the world, imaginations were stirred instantly and deeply. Differences of nationality and social status did not affect the response. In New York, Boston, Seattle, London, Sydney, Hobart, Auckland, Paris, Vienna—in hundreds of towns and villages throughout America, Europe, Asia and other parts of the world—there arose an insistent clamour for some means of conveyance to the fabulous El Dorado on the banks of the distant Sacramento River; and this demand grew steadily in volume.

The more adventurous left at once for California, the less venturesome waited only to settle their more urgent affairs, and the cautious tarried but to purchase what they regarded—or were induced by salesmen to regard— as necessities for such a daring enterprise. Before many weeks had passed thousands of people from Great Britain and Europe, all intent upon getting to the land of gold with the least possible delay, were pouring into the eastern seaboard of the United States to join the thousands of Americans who had formed a similar resolution.

By the beginning of 1849, from every part of the globe, tens of thousands of people of diverse character and background were on their way to, or about to leave for, California. There were business and professional men, clerks, mechanics, labourers, ne'er-do-wells, ex-jailbirds— as motley and varied a cross-section of humanity as it is possible to imagine, linked by a common belief that they were about to make their fortunes.

For a short time, as more and more people reached the Sacramento, Sutter prospered. Gold poured into his coffers. His horses, cattle and sheep, his beef and mutton, his blankets, shirts and hats, his groceries and brandy sold readily at high prices. But his virtual monopoly soon ended. Rival traders and shopkeepers appeared; his workmen, despite generous wage increases, deserted to try their luck at mining; squatters settled on his lands and laughed at him when he spoke of his Mexican grants. His livestock was stolen and slaughtered. His son, John junior, had laid out the town of Sacramento, a square mile beside the fort, but gamblers and saloon-keepers descended upon it and the mayor they elected scoffed at Sutter's pretensions of ownership.

Sutter appealed to the military governor, but was curtly reminded that the validity of his Spanish and Mexican grants was doubtful. For years, until his death in a Washington hotel room in June 1880, an impoverished Sutter fought vainly for compensation from the United States. All he ever received was a compassionate grant of 250 dollars a month, and on this small allowance he lived for the last decade of his life.

13

Marshall, whose casual discovery ruined Sutter, fared no better at the hands of the new arrivals. They jumped his claims and cheated him at every turn. When he appealed to the courts, judges were bribed and juries packed to deny him justice. He died in abject poverty in August 1885.

When the great influx began there were three principal routes from eastern America to California—one by sea, the second by sea and land, and the third wholly by land. All three were arduous and perilous. It was a matter of personal preference or convenience, or of geographical situation, as to which a man chose.

Despite its many hazards, the all-sea route was perhaps the least dangerous, and certainly it offered fewer discomforts. From the eastern seaports of the United States this route ran round Cape Horn or through Magellan Strait into the Pacific Ocean and thence to San Francisco. So great was the demand for passages that every type of craft was pressed hurriedly into service. Many of these vessels were scarcely seaworthy, and all, particularly in the first few hectic months, were dangerously overcrowded and shamefully under-provisioned. Even by the lax standards of the day, the gold-seekers made the passage under conditions of unbelievable privation and discomfort.

Many vessels sailed for San Francisco never to be seen or heard of again. Others, dismasted or disabled, leaking so badly that the pumps had to be continuously manned to keep them afloat, struggled into some port en route. There they might lie for weeks undergoing repairs or be condemned as unseaworthy, to the chagrin of their stranded passengers. Conditions in the stately Californian clippers, with their fine lines, their tall, tapering masts and their enormous spread of canvas, were but slightly better than in the older, smaller and slower vessels, for they also were overcrowded and in the rivalry to reach San Francisco in record time were always hard driven.

Even the best passages—such as the *Flying Cloud's* 89 days from New York in 1851, a feat she equalled three years later, or the *Flying Fish's* 98 days from Boston in 1851–2—were slow by modern standards. The average passage from New York or Boston to San Francisco of the fourteen extreme clippers that bettered 110 days in 1850 and 1851 was 104 days. Other vessels took as long as from 180 to 220 days on the passage, and one—a paddlewheel steamboat—300 days. The length of these longer passages was admittedly exceptional, but most vessels took at least 115 days—almost four months—to reach San Francisco from New York or Boston. The Cape Horn route was long, stormy and hazardous, and the fares were high; but while the gold fever persisted there was never a shortage of applicants for passages.

The sea and land route was via Panama, and it was this way that the first arrivals from the east came. From the eastern United States ports the gold-seekers travelled by steamer or sailing ship to Chagres, a few miles from Aspinwall, as Colon was then named. They then crossed the isthmus of Panama and picked up another ship on the Pacific side.

The United States Mail Steamship Company had been formed in 1847, after the award by the U.S. Navy Department of a contract for a subsidized coastwise service between New York and New Orleans. This service was by way of Charleston, Savannah and Havana, and the contract provided that each month one vessel should go on from Havana to Chagres with the New York and New Orleans mails. The chartered 1,000-ton steamship *Falcon* instituted the service to Chagres when she sailed from New York on 5th December 1848. So heavy was the demand for passages that by 1852 the company was employing nine steamships.

The railway across the isthmus of Panama was not completed until 1855. Before then, travellers crossed from Chagres to Panama by canoe, muleback or on foot. The distance was comparatively short, but the route lay across low mountains and through swamps and jungles, inhabited by malaria-carrying mosquitoes and poisonous reptiles. Cholera and yellow fever took their toll, too.

From Panama the steamers of the Pacific Mail Line, which also had been formed in 1847 following the award of a government subsidy, ran to San Francisco. The line's three new steamships—the *California*, the *Panama* and the *Oregon*—were completed in the final quarter of 1848, and on 6th October the 1,085-ton, 200-feet-long wooden paddlewheeler *California* sailed from New York for San Francisco. She had accommodation for 50 cabin and 150 steerage passengers. When she left New York to inaugurate the service between Panama and Puget Sound she carried only seven passengers, none of whom was bound for the west coast.

News of the gold strike reached New York after the *California's* departure. Hastily, a crowd of would-be miners sailed for Chagres, determined to be at Panama by the time the *California* arrived. Thus, when she entered Panama no fewer than 1,500 people clamoured to get aboard her. With extra berths erected, she was able to accommodate 365 passengers in addition to a crew of 36. The *California* sailed from Panama with this number on 30th January 1849. She reached San Francisco on 28th February.

The *Oregon* and the *Panama* later joined the *California* in the Panama–San Francisco service. Other steamships were chartered, while rival companies sprang into being. However, the demand for passages could scarcely be met, and many travellers were compelled to complete their journey to San Francisco by fishing-boat, whaler or even dug-out canoe.

The all-land route was the most difficult and dangerous. The long trek across the United States on horseback or in the famed 'prairie schooner' involved crossing the far-flung plains, the Rocky Mountains, the almost unexplored desert basin and the mighty range of the Sierra Nevada. The natural obstacles were many and formidable, and

James Marshall, who first discovered gold at
Sutter's Mill on the Sacramento River, California
(New York Public Library)

Sydney in 1851, by W. S. Hatton (From the copy in the Dixson Library, Sydney)

they were rendered more hazardous by the resistance of the Red Indians to the white man's westward advance.

Later, two additional routes to California were opened, but they were of minor importance. The first lay across central Mexico, the second over the isthmus of Tehuantepec in Nicaragua. A through service via Nicaragua was opened in July 1851 by Commodore Cornelius Vanderbilt's Accessory Transit Company. This route was five hundred miles shorter than that via Panama and had only twelve miles of portage by way of the San Juan River and Lake Nicaragua. However, neither route was as popular as those established earlier, and the number of travellers who used them to reach California was small.

But all the Forty-Niners and their successors did not start their journey from America's eastern states. Many came from foreign lands without touching an American port until they entered San Francisco. From Britain, Europe, China, Australia, New Zealand, Singapore, Hong Kong and the many islands studding the vast Pacific, vessels of many sizes voyaged to San Francisco with their loads of eager passengers. In numbers these immigrants were far fewer than those who came from the east, but the perils and privations they faced were as great and the adventures they experienced as strange.

We who are accustomed to travel speedily and comfortably in modern liners have no conception of the agony of being tossed about for months on end in a small, crowded sailing ship. The conditions and means of travel in the middle of the nineteenth century were so different from what they are today that we are surprised men and women of even the most adventurous disposition should have crossed the world in tens of thousands, let alone that the journey should have been undertaken by many thousands who hitherto had led comfortable, uneventful and often sheltered lives. Nothing illustrates more forcibly the lure of fortune than the way in which all these people voluntarily relinquished their steady livings to face the hardships and perils of gold-seeking.

It will never be known how many people set out for the goldfields or how many arrived. There is no lack of estimates, but at best these are only calculated guesses. They vary widely, ranging from an annual average of around seventy thousand to at least double that figure. In 1849, when no fewer than 775 vessels sailed for San Francisco from America's Atlantic ports alone, 91,405 passengers disembarked at San Francisco from all parts of the world[2] and perhaps another forty thousand struggled forward along the overland trail. The following year slightly more than thirty-six thousand passengers landed at San Francisco and about the same number came overland.[3]

Between 1848 and 1851 inclusive, the number of passengers reaching California from the Atlantic states totalled 412,942, of whom 241,522 came by way of Panama or Nicaragua. For the three years 1849–51 the annual average of arrivals was 141,350, of whom 80,190 came by sea and 61,160 by land.[4] To these figures must be added those who reached California without touching the Atlantic seaboard of the United States.

Reliable figures of the amount of freight brought to San Francisco are equally elusive, but it has been calculated that between 1848 and 1851 no less than 47,000 tons came by way of Panama alone.[5] Almost every vessel entering the Golden Gate was crammed with goods as well as passengers, and when the rush was at its height freight rates were such that a single passage from New York or Boston to San Francisco might gross a shipowner the total cost of a Californian clipper. Except for goods that could not be sold on a market quickly overstocked and which therefore were re-exported, the only return cargo was gold. Immense quantities were shipped. By 1851 over 138,000,000 dollars' worth had been carried across the Panama isthmus,[6] while the Pacific Mail Steamship Company alone had shipped nearly 122,000,000 dollars' worth by the end of 1852.[7]

No single event in its history has had such immediate

and lasting effects upon California as the gold rush. In a few years it brought an expansion in population, commerce, agriculture and industry and the provision of transportation facilities which, under normal circumstances, might not have been achieved in three decades or more. It abruptly ended the physical and intellectual isolation of California, it smoothed the transfer of sovereignty from Mexico to the United States, it speeded up the establishment of an effective system of administration, and it shifted the political and intellectual centre of the state from Los Angeles to San Francisco. The influx of foreigners infused into its racial structure a cosmopolitanism that otherwise might well have been absent.

The great tide of immigration that followed in the wake of Marshall's discovery left practically untouched the long coastal plain running south from Monterey to the Mexican border. In this cattle country of great ranchos, little increase in population took place, new cities and towns did not spring overnight into robust life, and except for the movement to the mines and the boom conditions created by high beef prices, the life and customs of the Spanish Californians were unaffected.

But north of Monterey the changes were dramatic and revolutionary. As Robert Cleland has said: 'The huge immigration which poured into northern California from every quarter of the globe overwhelmed the native population, transformed drowsy adobe pueblos into sprawling, cosmopolitan cities, and supplanted the simple agrarian life of the Spanish Californians with a frontier society of the most explosive type.'[8]

In 1848 California had a population of about 15,000 people of Spanish-Mexican or Anglo-Saxon descent. By 1850 the population had swollen to nearly 100,000, by 1852 it had leapt to 224,435, and by 1860 another census showed it had grown to 380,015. San Francisco, which in 1848 had 800 inhabitants, two wharves and two hotels, within two years became a rumbustious wood and canvas city of almost 40,000 souls, its streets lined with saloons, brothels and gambling dens. Other cities—Sacramento, Stockton, Grass Valley, Marysville—were added to the map. In a few weeks they became bustling and lusty cities, with populations ranging from 3,000 to 7,000 people. Life was hard, rough and exciting, frequently violently so. The miners won enormous quantities of gold and spent it recklessly in the saloons and dives. The Californian State Mining Bureau has computed that ten million dollars' worth of gold was won in 1849, forty-one millions in 1850, seventy-six millions the following year and eighty-one millions in 1852.[9] Indeed, the five years of the gold rush advanced Californian progress by at least thirty to fifty years.

For many vessels the passage to California was their last. They never sailed again. Immediately they dropped anchor in the wide expanse of San Francisco Bay officers and men deserted to search for gold. Vessels of every type of rig and of every nationality rotted at their moorings, were driven ashore and wrecked in gales or were converted into hotels, warehouses, stores, gambling saloons or other buildings, usually being beached for this purpose. The comparatively few vessels to sail out into the Pacific again, apart from those trading more or less regularly to Panama, were each taken to sea by a handful of men. These skeleton crews, recruited by ruffianly crimps or by the lure of exceptionally high wages, navigated the vessels to the Sandwich Islands, China or some other place where a full crew might be engaged at normal wages.

Among the gold-seekers who did not touch an American port until they sailed into San Francisco Bay were the men, women and children who came from Australia and New Zealand. Word of Marshall's rich find reached these distant British colonies in the last days of 1848, and the forerunners of the fleet that eventually crossed the Pacific were racing for San Francisco before the new year was a month old.

Australia and New Zealand were undeveloped and

sparsely populated, and their inhabitants were mostly poor. The total population of the Australian colonies, including male and female convicts under sentence of transportation, was around four hundred thousand. In New Zealand there were fewer than thirty thousand white people. Needing manpower, both countries had been actively fostering migration. Yet many shiploads of Australians and New Zealanders sailed to California in 1849–50.

In Australia the Californian trade centred at Sydney, whose shipowners and merchants were more enterprising than those at other Australian ports. They dispatched more vessels from Sydney in 1849 than sailed from the rest of Australia. Next to Sydney, the ports most active in the trade were Hobart and Launceston, in Van Diemen's Land, as Tasmania was then still called. However, in Tasmania the height of the rush came much later than in Sydney. Auckland was the headquarters of the Californian trade in New Zealand, and few vessels sailed from other ports.

An economic recession gave a fillip to the trade. With local markets lifeless and unprofitable, merchants were more inclined to risk the gamble of consigning goods for sale in California than they would have been had the local demand been brisk. Unemployment prevented many from raising the fare to California, but provided many more with a motive for getting to San Francisco. There was a feeling among a large section of the community that the goldfields along the Sacramento presented brighter prospects of steady employment than were to be found in Australia. Another factor, the effect of which is difficult to determine, was the desire of many people to emigrate to a country free from the taint of convictism. The trade recession was not confined to the Antipodes. In India, China and elsewhere few profitable cargoes were offering and many 'seeking' ships, the ocean tramps of those days of sail, preferred to sail for San Francisco rather than waste weeks or months searching elsewhere for cargoes. The competition of these ocean-going vessels kept passenger and freight rates low.

Australia's gold fleet for California was thus a motley one. The big ships which had brought out prisoners or free immigrants, or which had carried cargo only, competed with small coastal vessels for passengers and cargoes. Some of the latter vessels were tiny craft of but a few tons' burthen. Yet, large or small, all set out gallantly on the long haul across the Pacific, an ocean which so often belies its name. It says much for the staunchness of all these vessels and for the navigational ability of their masters that only a few failed to reach their destination.

The tide of emigration from Australia and New Zealand ended as abruptly as it had begun. It was ironical that so many hundreds set out to make their fortunes on the goldfields when only a few months later Australia herself was to become the magnet for the world's gold-seekers. In 1851 gold was discovered in New South Wales, followed by rich finds in Victoria. No longer did men clamour for passages to California. Instead, a steady stream of ships began to reach Australia, many of them from San Francisco and all loaded with optimistic miners. Soon the masts of idle, deserted ships formed a leafless forest in Port Phillip Bay, as earlier they had done in San Francisco. The brief, crowded, colourful life of Australia's gold fleet for California was ended.

2 *THE NEWS COMES TO AUSTRALIA*

I N AUSTRALIA the first announcement of the Californian gold discovery was published on 23rd December 1848, when Sydney's only daily newspaper, the *Sydney Morning Herald*, printed extracts from a Honolulu newspaper, the *Polynesian*. The overland mail carried the news to Melbourne, where it was published on 30th December. It reached Hobart and Adelaide by coastal sailing vessel, the first announcement being printed in Hobart on 9th January 1849, and in Adelaide on 27th January.

Word of Marshall's find had reached New Zealand several weeks earlier. Late in November the American whaler *Balfour* had put into the Bay of Islands to land two passengers from Tahiti. Her master or passengers had brought some newspapers published at the Sandwich Islands, as the Hawaiian group was then called. These newspapers contained reports of the Californian discoveries, and word of the gold strike circulated quickly among the permanent and transient residents of the Bay of Islands, a famed rendezvous of whalers.

From the Bay of Islands the news travelled to Auckland, where it appeared in the *New Zealander* of 2nd December. It reached Wellington, at the opposite end of the North Island, by the barque *Cornelia* on Sunday, 10th December, but so intermittent were communications between the North and South Islands that it was not published in Dunedin, away to the south, until 7th March, 1849.

A certain amount of mystery surrounds the receipt of the first news in Australia. Three days before the *Sydney Morning Herald's* announcement of 23rd December, the schooner *Plymouth* had arrived from the Sandwich Islands, which she had left on 9th November. A schooner of 85 tons, built principally of teak, the *Plymouth* originally had been on the British register as the *Sri Singapura*. She had arrived at Honolulu on 5th September 1848 from Hong Kong with a cargo of merchandise from the Bonin Islands consigned to Henry Skinner and Company. Her master, Charles Campbell, died before the month was out and was buried in Nuuanu Valley cemetery. On 27th September, presumably because of Campbell's death, the *Sri Singapura* was sold at public auction by F. W. Thompason. She was purchased for 2,500 dollars by William Paty, who renamed her the *Plymouth* and placed her on the Hawaiian register.[1] George H. Gould was appointed her commander and, loaded with twenty tons of molasses and five tons of sugar—a surprisingly small cargo—she was dispatched to Sydney.[2]

Those aboard the *Plymouth* knew of the gold discoveries in California. Indeed, Captain Gould actually had in his possession a keg of Californian gold as well as some November issues of the *Polynesian* containing the latest news from the gold region. But he said nothing to the *Herald's* shipping reporter of the stirring events in California, and in reporting the *Plymouth's* arrival that newspaper said: 'She brings no news from the islands.' Undoubtedly, Captain Gould's silence was deliberate.

We may guess that the *Plymouth* had been dispatched from Honolulu to carry news of Marshall's discovery to somebody in Sydney, and all the evidence points to this somebody being the prominent mercantile firm of Montefiore, Graham and Company. When the *Plymouth* sailed from Sydney for San Francisco on 8th January, her cargo was consigned entirely by this firm. They also consigned a cargo to San Francisco in the *Despatch*, which they evidently chartered and in which Mr. F. Montefiore,

Captain John Sutter, at whose mill the first gold was found
(New York Public Library)

The schooner or brigantine *Deborah*, the first vessel to sail from New Zealand to California in 1849
(From a painting in the Alexander Turnbull Library, Wellington)

a member of the firm, travelled as supercargo. We may surmise that Gould's silence was designed to give Montefiore, Graham and Company an advantage in purchasing a cargo for California and in chartering another vessel to follow the *Plymouth* thither.

Probably Gould imagined there was little chance of his scheme going awry. Except for the mate, the *Plymouth's* crew were South Sea islanders. Their knowledge of English was confined to a few words of pidgin. It was unlikely that the news would be disseminated by them, even if they were aware of it or appreciated its significance, and the mate could be trusted to keep his mouth closed. Gould knew, moreover, that when he had left Honolulu no other vessel had been on the berth there for Sydney and it was improbable that any vessel would arrive direct from San Francisco. To him it must have seemed a certainty that his principals would be able to purchase a cargo for California before word of Marshall's find sent prices up or brought competitors into the field. He could scarcely have foreseen that the *Plymouth* would be followed into Sydney Harbour by two vessels from New Zealand and that one of these would bring news of the gold discoveries.

On 21st December, according to an official record of arrivals, but the previous day—that is, the same day as the *Plymouth* arrived—according to the *Sydney Morning Herald*, the brig *Phantom* reached Sydney from Auckland,[3] and on 22nd December the schooner *Despatch* arrived from Otago.[4]

The 158-ton *Phantom*, a well-known inter-colonial trader, had been built at Brucehaven, in the Scottish county of Fife, in 1841 and four years later had been registered at Calcutta. On a voyage to Australia from India she was purchased by the Sydney merchant, Thomas Woolley, in whose name she was registered at Sydney on 22nd January 1847. She evidently cost him a considerable sum, as the day after he registered her he raised a mortgage of £2,000 on her. She was a single-decked vessel, with a sunk poop and topgallant forecastle, and was rigged as a two-mast schooner. She had a length of 85.4 feet, with a beam of 22.5 and a depth of 11.0 feet, and was styled a 'Packet Brig' by her agents, Messrs. Sheppard and Alger, who called their premises at 470 George Street the Packet Office. The *Phantom* was commanded by Henry Thomas Fox, and on this passage from New Zealand she carried eight cabin and thirty-seven or thirty-eight steerage passengers, in addition to a crew of fifteen. She had on board at least sixty people.[5]

The official notice of the *Phantom's* arrival states she had sailed from Auckland on 3rd December and from Kawau on the same day. The *Herald* agrees she had left Auckland on 3rd December, but reports her departure from Kawau as having taken place on the 4th and adds that she had left the Bay of Islands on the 8th. Therefore, the *Phantom* had sailed from Auckland the day after the *New Zealander's* publication of the news from California and, if the *Herald's* report is correct, had called at the Bay of Islands, where, no doubt, the gold strike was a lively topic of conversation.

On the other hand, the *Despatch* could not have been in possession of the news. This 139-ton, two-mast schooner-brig had left Otago on 30th November.[6] She had not called at any port and had not spoken any vessel which knew about the goldfields.

Why, then, did the *Herald* not publish the announcement until 23rd December? Beyond doubt, the answer seems to be that, like Gould, Captain Fox, of the *Phantom*, made no mention of California on his arrival. He was interviewed by Thomas Hinigan, the *Herald's* shipping reporter, and recounted to him the story of the *Phantom's* stormy passage to New Zealand in November, when a sudden squall had thrown her on her beam ends and had carried away every stitch of canvas except her foretopmast staysail. Fox also gave Hinigan details of the arrivals and departures of vessels at Auckland and the names of American whalers that had touched at the Bay of Islands.

All this information the *Herald* published next day, on the 22nd.[7] Whether Fox's silence was deliberate or inadvertent must be a matter of conjecture, but in view of the number of passengers in the *Phantom* he could scarcely have hoped to suppress the momentous news for any length of time. The passengers began to talk about it as soon as they were ashore, and the news, spreading rapidly by word of mouth and as copies of the *New Zealander* were handed round, quickly reached the *Herald* office, with the result that it was published next day.

The yellowed pages of the *Melbourne Daily News* confirm this interpretation of events. This newspaper said the news of the finding of 'glittering, glorious gold' in vast quantities and great purity in California came 'from Polynesian papers received in New Zealand up to last July.'[8] The very phrase 'glittering, glorious gold' was borrowed from the *New Zealander*, which had stated: 'Gold, glittering glorious gold has been discovered in amazing quantities and of the utmost purity in California.' Since no vessels had arrived recently at Melbourne from New Zealand, the news obviously had come from Sydney.

Gould, now that the news was out, became communicative. He produced a bundle of Sandwich Island newspapers to 4th November, and from these the *Herald* culled extracts which it published in its Boxing Day issue. The existence of Gould's keg of gold, however, was not disclosed in the *Herald* until 30th December.

'It is stated by those who are judges to be of the finest description,' said the *Herald*; 'it is in grains of pure gold, some of them larger than a pea. A great deal of it has been sold at seventy shillings an ounce, at which price one firm in Sydney has purchased a thousand ounces for the purpose of sending it to England as a remittance. It is very probable that some more of it may find its way to Sydney in exchange for beef and flour, of which the Californians are so much in need.'

Yet the cargo taken by the *Plymouth* to San Francisco seems not to have been of great value. It consisted of 2

27

quarter casks of rum, 50 barrels of pork, 156 cases and 75 packages of oilman's stores, 74 packages of ironmongery, 27 cases and 2 quarter cases of wine, 56 packages of haberdashery, 1 tin of biscuit, 7 hundredweight of hams and 6 quarter casks of brandy.

To a generation accustomed to the bold, large-type headings and elaborate display of the modern popular press, the announcement of Marshall's discovery in the various Australian newspapers appears curiously dull, uninteresting and unexciting. Looking at these brittle pages, it is difficult to appreciate that the news so unobtrusively announced was to trigger off a stampede from all parts of the world.

In its first publication, the *Herald* used a single seven-point heading, set in roman—that is, a light instead of a bold—type :

NEW GOLD MINE

The *Melbourne Daily News*, being an evening newspaper, was less conservative. It employed ten-point roman type and its heading read :

MONSTER GOLD MINES

But this is the way important news was presented just over a century ago, and despite the inconspicuous presentation these reports fired the imaginations of Australia's few inhabitants.

THE INTERVENTION of Christmas and the New Year delayed public reaction to the news. During the brief holiday season the subject was widely discussed, however, and among all sections of the community the advisability of emigrating to California was wordily canvassed. The sceptics, fairly numerous at first, dwindled to a handful, and as early as 4th January the *Herald* alluded to their discomfiture.

'When the first notice of the gold mines appeared in the *Herald*, said that newspaper, 'many persons looked upon it as a hoax; but the fact of large quantities of gold having actually arrived in Sydney and been purchased at £3. 7s. and £3. 10s. per ounce soon convinced the most unbelieving of the truth of the statements which had been made. We believe several persons are going to send provisions to California, and if they arrive there before shipments from the United States, immense profits will be made.'

Vessels now began to be placed on the berth for California. The *Plymouth* was scheduled to sail on 7th January and the smaller *Despatch*, which had been built at Jersey in 1838 and was owned by two Sydney master mariners, William Francis Plant and Andrew Bliss, was reported to have been chartered to sail in the course of a fortnight.[1] On 5th January the first unchartered vessel was advertised. She was the 480-ton barque *Eleanor Lancaster*, belonging to the London shipowner Robert Brooks, and commanded by Francis W. Lodge. Within a few days the 182-ton brig *Louisa*, the 121-ton schooner *Deborah*, whose master was Andrew Bliss, part owner of the *Despatch*, and the 'clipper barque' *Lindsays* were also advertised for California.

In Hobart, Melbourne and Adelaide the response was less spontaneous. A few vessels were advertised promptly for San Francisco, but when passengers did not come forward in any numbers and freight was offered only in small quantities most of these vessels were withdrawn. The agents, merchants and shipowners, more conservative than their counterparts in Sydney, made no attempt to whip up enthusiasm for California by skilful propaganda and forceful canvassing. Their negative attitude was in striking contrast to the dynamic conduct of the shipping interests at Port Jackson, where no opportunity to encourage emigration and the shipment of goods to California was overlooked. Indeed, in their eagerness the Sydney men were guilty of some misrepresentation. Their descriptions of the prospects and conditions on the goldfields were as grossly exaggerated as were the sailing qualities, the standard of provisioning and the degree of comfort in the accommodation of their vessels.

While the gold craze lasted the agents of the first vessels advertised from Sydney were the most active in procuring ships for California and in filling them with passengers and cargo. They advertised extensively in the newspapers and by means of handbills, the latter being distributed in thousands and soon becoming a familiar sight on posts, houses and fences.

The agent for the *Eleanor Lancaster* was Robert Towns, a master mariner who, having made a number of voyages between England and Australia, had settled in Sydney in 1842 as a merchant, shipowner and shipping agent. 'Lodge's was a seeking ship,' he wrote Robert Brooks on 17th January, 'and had no good prospect in India or China. I recommended him to lay on for that quarter

[California]—it is all on his road—seeking on the west coast.'[2]

Although he induced Captain Lodge to sail for San Francisco, Towns professed repeatedly to be sceptical of the fortunes to be won by trading ventures to California and advised caution to friends contemplating journeying to the diggings. Yet he remained throughout closely and actively associated with the Californian trade. He acted as agent for many ships that sailed for San Francisco and he dispatched some of his own vessels thither, besides chartering others. He also shipped a variety of goods in speculative trading ventures, sometimes, it would seem, against his better judgment. The majority of the vessels owned by Captain Towns were old and he spent relatively little on their upkeep, with the result that the spot where they were moored in Sydney Harbour was facetiously known as 'Rotten Row'.[3] But Towns sent some of these vessels across the Pacific and induced his friends and customers to dispatch goods in them.

Like Towns, John MacNamara was a shipowner as well as an agent. He owned the *Louisa*, which previously he had employed in the coastal trade. She had been built at Southtown, Suffolk, in 1834 and had been purchased by MacNamara nine years later. He also owned two particularly well known local traders, the Irish-built *Emma* and the Sydney-built *Wild Irish Girl*, both small brigs. But, except for the *Louisa*, the vessels he dispatched to California were mostly, if not all, owned by others, although he may have chartered some of them.

R. T. Ford, whose place of business was at 8 Bridge Street, was agent for the *Deborah*. A shipping and customs agent, his activities had been confined principally to the coastal trades. Apparently he neither owned nor chartered any of the vessels he advertised for California, and he does not seem to have gambled with shipments of cargo to San Francisco. His interest in the Californian trade was simply that of an agent.

The firm of Sheppard and Alger, who loaded the

Lindsays in association with J. H. Levien, was prominent in the management of vessels running between Sydney, Melbourne, Hobart and Adelaide, but especially in the so-called packets linking Sydney and Hobart. Their business was principally in acting as agents for overseas and local vessels and was an extensive and flourishing one. They were particularly proud of their 'packet' connection, which they emphasized in all their advertising. Indeed, it was this packet connection which induced them to lay on the first line of packets from Sydney to California—a venture which was not crowned with the success they had hoped.

With ships advertised for California, merchants and traders began to push their wares. The first advertisements of goods for sale specifically directed towards Californian traders and immigrants appeared in the *Herald* on 8th January. J. S. Harrison, wholesale butter, bacon and cheese monger, whose market was located at 26–28 George Street, headed his advertisement with the word 'California', and drew the attention of merchants to the fact that he had 'a large and superior stock on hand'. However, Harrison himself was succumbing to the gold fever and announced that, if sufficient inducement offered, he would 'undertake to proceed to California as supercargo'[3]. One, Elliott, who conducted a 'Shipping Depot' in Lower George Street, likewise headed his advertisement, 'California'. He offered for sale preserved meats and soups in small tins, stating they were warranted to keep in any climate and were 'particularly suited for the starvation districts of California'.[4]

In the weeks that followed, additional ships were placed on the berth for California and a much wider range of goods was offered as being suitable for the goldfields. Before long, the latter included carbines, charts of the North Pacific (advertised under the heading of 'The Way to California'), foodstuffs of all sorts, blankets, boots, shoes, nails, axes, flag baskets ('expressly sent out for mining purposes'), and many other articles described as suitable for the Californian market or as indispensable necessities for those going to the diggings.

Trade in Sydney, which had been at a low ebb, began to recover. 'Trade and business never was known to be so dull,' Towns wrote a Calcutta firm on 29th November 1848, 'and I see very little prospect of improvement. The late low prices for our ruling staple in the home market, wool, has thrown us out of all calculation'. Next day he advised a Manila house that 'business of all kinds is at a stand', and on 22nd December reported: 'We have no improvement in business.'[5] Writing to Captain Goldsmith of Hobart, on 23rd December, the very day on which the *Herald* announced the gold discovery, Towns said: 'I am glad to see your freights are something better than we have here—£3 for tallow, £4. 10s. for oil and 1d. per lb. for wool, and no prospect of any advance on these rates . . . it's miserable work loading ships at such rates. Stevedores have lowered the rates for stowage to 4s. 6d. per bale—it was 5s. . . . This colony is in a shocking state from the late low prices of wool, the amount to refund is very serious—it will require years to bring the settlers sound.'[6]

R. Harnett, a broker of 1 Jamieson Street, who furnished the *Herald* with regular reports on the state of trade, took an equally pessimistic view at the year's end. He reported that 'the quantity of goods thrown into the market being far more than can at present be taken off deters the buyers from coming forward; prices have in many instances ruled exceedingly low'. Three weeks later he was more optimistic. 'Several vessels having been laid on for the coast of California,' he reported, 'merchandise to a considerable amount is being shipped, principally of such goods as are abundant in this market; but many large packets have been taken, consisting of oilmen's stores, salt provisions, spirits, etc., and a large quantity of drapery goods have also been purchased for the same destination. The consequence is, a very brisk trade has been done for the last few days and our market is therefore much relieved by such a continued run upon it. The demand has been so general that every branch of trade has felt it, and stocks are so much reduced as to leave us very bare of many articles.'[7]

Viewing the market from the point of view of his own business, Towns was less enthusiastic. 'We are in a most deplorable state as to general business,' he wrote on 9th February 1849, and a fortnight later he asserted: 'Business of all kinds is fearfully dull. Tea, sugar and such articles of consumption selling much under import prices . . . generally speaking a heavy gloom hangs over every branch of business . . . to crown all we have every prospect of a drought.' Yet the dour Towns admitted that Californian shipments had effected some improvement in certain lines. 'A few drapery goods are getting scarce,' he told a correspondent on 9th February, 'and everything in the soft goods line is progressing well.' On 22nd February he remarked that 'drapery goods in some articles are paying well'.[8]

While at least some traders were getting rid of their surplus goods, the shipping agents were busy booking passengers for the long voyage across the Pacific. If the rates advertised by Captain Towns for the *Eleanor Lancaster* may be taken as representative, a cabin passage from Sydney to San Francisco in January cost £30 and a steerage passage £10. Towns, in answering inquiries from East Maitland and Singleton regarding passages, insisted upon these fares. 'The rates published in the "Sydney Morning Herald" are the terms,' he informed one prospective passenger.[9] Most agents, however, preferred not to quote actual fares in their advertising. It may be inferred from this omission that they were determined to compel would-be passengers to visit their offices because their rates were elastic. When an inquirer came in, they drove the best bargain they could. Most agents, no doubt, filled up vacant berths at the last moment at reduced fares.

There was no lack of people wanting to go to California,

and prospective passengers crowded the shipping offices. But if the unemployment that had characterized the trade recession was responsible for this, it also was responsible for many of the inquirers being unable to pay for their passages. Some sought to work their passages, wholly or in part. Thus, one man offered to serve as carpenter in the *Eleanor Lancaster*, only to be told by Towns that the vessel already had a carpenter and therefore no allowance on that account could be deducted from the steerage fare of £10.[10]

From all these applicants the persuasive agents had little difficulty in extracting deposits on the understanding that the balance should be paid before the vessel sailed. Shortly before the scheduled day of sailing, the agent advertised that outstanding balances must be paid by a certain date or the berths be forfeited. Often some passengers had to default, and on the eve of a ship's departure several berths, cabin and steerage, might be advertised as still available. The most fortunate were those who had booked on a vessel for which the demand exceeded the number of berths. Those who had been unable to earn, borrow or steal the amount still owing on their passage did not then forfeit their deposits, as their reservations were transferred to the next vessel which that particular agent was dispatching.

According to the *Eleanor Lancaster's* advertisement, the freight rate to San Francisco was £5 per ton on weight or measurement. 'The lowest rate at which we are taking small parcels is £5 per ton, but for thirty tons deadweight we will say £4 per ton,' Towns informed one man.[11] Some shipowners and agents shipped goods on their own account, but most vessels sailed with cargoes consigned by a number of merchants and traders and by passengers. Towns, besides being prepared to reduce freight rates on larger consignments, offered an additional service to shippers. On 8th January he announced that 'a gentleman well acquainted with the Spanish language and trade of the coast' would proceed in the *Eleanor Lancaster* if

35

sufficient inducements offered to his consignment. The response evidently was satisfactory, and four days later J. C. Catton, who had been forced to relinquish his position as a clerk in the office of Rowand, McNab and Company when that firm of merchants had been compelled to cease business because of the failure of their Liverpool house, announced that he was proceeding in the *Eleanor Lancaster* as supercargo.[12]

Meanwhile, in Hobart the schooner *Eliza*, the brigantine *John Bull* and the barque *Marianne* were advertised for California. A local merchant, Captain Andrew Haig, who before settling in Hobart had made many voyages to Tasmania from England in command of the ship *Sir John Rae Reid*, offered to charter a vessel if a sufficient number of passengers came forward. 'A steerage passage for an adult would be £25,' his advertisement stated, 'a cabin passage £50, and families pro rata, for which good accommodation and food would be guaranteed.'[13]

However, in Tasmania only a little freight offered and few passengers. Perhaps the fares were too high. According to Haig's offer, it cost £20 more for a cabin and £15 more for a steerage passage from Hobart than from Sydney. It was cheaper for a Tasmanian to go by way of Sydney, since fares between Sydney and Hobart were low—£5 for a cabin and half that for a steerage passage. So, in the event, only the *Eliza* sailed from Hobart for San Francisco and she carried no passengers.

In Melbourne the response, from a shipowner's point of view, was even more unsatisfactory. The barque *Thomas Lowry*, which had been connected with the Australian trade for many years, was the first vessel placed on the berth for California, but eventually, in ballast and without passengers, she sailed for Hong Kong. The schooner *Minerva* likewise failed to obtain any passengers for San Francisco and went instead to Sydney. Not until the end of June did the first vessel sail for California from Melbourne.[14]

As with Hobart, however, Melbourne's apathy may

have been less real than appeared on the surface. Victorian residents may well have decided that the quickest and cheapest route to the goldfields was by way of Sydney. Several small vessels traded regularly between Melbourne and Sydney, and fares, particularly in the steerage, were low. We know that J. McEachern, a former editor of the *Port Phillip Patriot*, and J. Mawhood, a shipping reporter, both journeyed from Melbourne to Sydney and left the latter port in January for San Francisco.[15] Many others may have chosen the same route.

Adelaide, belatedly receiving the news, had much the same experience as Melbourne and Hobart. Three vessels were promptly advertised for California, but there was no rush of passengers and it was many weeks before the first vessel sailed from Port Adelaide.[16]

4 RACING ACROSS THE PACIFIC

B Y THE END of January 1849, seven vessels—six
from Sydney and one from Hobart—had sailed
from Australia for San Francisco. Aboard them
were ninety-three passengers, including six women and
four children. Most of these were in two vessels, the
barque *Eleanor Lancaster* carrying fifty-two and the brig
Louisa thirty-four.

Whether they carried passengers or not, all these
vessels were loaded to capacity with general cargo. Thus,
Montefiore, Graham and Company shipped in the
Despatch 200 iron pots, 245 casks of beer, 82 bundles and
10 packages of hardware goods, 13 packages of drugs, 50
bags of flour, 40 boxes of soap, 156 cases and 10 boxes of
oilmen's stores, and tea, champagne, sherry, haberdashery, boots, shoes, hops and other articles in varying
quantities. The brig *William Hill* carried spirits, beer,
tobacco, mustard, spades, saddlery, oil, paint, pickles,
beef, butter, pork, wine and other articles, mostly in small
quantities of each. The barque *Lindsays* was loaded with
spirits, tobacco, rice, tea, coffee, suet, soups, split peas,
lard, pork, tongues, grindstones, castor oil, corks, pipes,
paint brushes, looking-glasses, boots, shoes, windowglass,
nails, guns, paint, rope, copper, camp ovens, iron pots,
and candles. These cargoes were typical.

Writing to Robert Brooks a few days before the *Eleanor
Lancaster* sailed, Towns said she carried 'passengers and

some few tons of cargo' and 'makes rather more than £700, little or no expense, no detention'.[1] The Passengers' Act obliged any vessel with more than fifty souls aboard to carry a surgeon, but the astute Towns had engaged a medical man so anxious to get to California that he was willing to serve without salary. Indeed, Dr. Silver paid £10 for his passage. He agreed to act as surgeon without pay but, according to the *Eleanor Lancaster's* movements after her arrival, he was to receive a passage from San Francisco to England or back to Australia. However, he might leave the vessel at any port if he so chose.[2]

The route from Australia to San Francisco depended upon two factors—firstly, the direction of the wind on leaving port and, secondly, the need to replenish water or provisions. This latter consideration necessitated some ships calling at one or more intermediate ports, usually in New Zealand, Tahiti or Hawaii.

At the time of the Californian gold rush Lieutenant Matthew Fontaine Maury's work in charting the winds and currents of the Pacific and his advocacy of Great Circle sailing were already widely known, although he did not publish his *Sailing Directions* until 1851. This United States naval officer's researches into the best sailing routes in the Pacific were not to be completed for another fifteen or twenty years, but around the half-century the winds and currents were much better understood by the general run of sea captains than even a decade earlier. At least, it was fairly widely appreciated that there existed three belts of calms and variable winds —the latitudes of Capricorn and of Cancer and the equator, with the south-east trades below and the north-east trades above the equator.

Moreover, Australian shipmasters had accumulated a body of weather lore peculiarly their own. For fifty years they had been sailing to Tahiti and Hawaii—the Navigator Islands and the Sandwich Islands, as they were commonly called at the time. They had gone there at first in search of pork and later to procure coconut oil, beche-de-mer, sandalwood and other island products, while whalers had been frequent callers at these islands to refresh or to repair their ships. On the other hand, there had been few passages from Australia to California.

San Francisco-bound vessels strove to run to New Zealand so as to pass through Cook Strait, but if the wind was foul for a direct passage across the Tasman, as it often was, they laid a course to pass to the north or to the south of New Zealand. Then they made easting to the southward of 40°S. before hauling up north for Tahiti or standing north-east into the south-east trades to run through the trade-wind belts to reach the westerlies for a direct passage to San Francisco. Honolulu was approached from the eastward because of the set of the equatorial current and to make the most of the wind and, the Hawaiian Islands lying in the belt of the trades, it was necessary, when sailing from there to San Francisco, to run north to reach the westerlies. Off the Californian coast itself, prevailing northerly winds, a current setting to the south and sudden fogs presented distinct navigational hazards.

Of the first seven vessels to sail for California only two were Australian-built. The brig *William Hill* had been built at the Clarence River, N.S.W., by William Phillips in 1847 for a Sydney merchant, Edward Smith Hill. Obviously she was named for a member of her owner's family, and when she sailed E. S. Hill and W. Hill were two of her three passengers. The other Australian-built vessel was the schooner *Eliza*, which sailed from Hobart. She had been constructed by convicts at Port Arthur for the Government in 1834, but eventually had come into private ownership.[3]

The *Eleanor Lancaster*, which left Sydney on 21st January, was the first of the seven vessels to arrive at San Francisco. She anchored there on 2nd April, after a passage of seventy-one days. The *William Hill*, which was the only other vessel to make a direct passage, took eighty-eight days. The *Plymouth*, the first vessel to sail, and the *Despatch* called at both Tahiti and Honolulu, and the *Louisa*, the *Eliza* and the *Lindsays* went via Honolulu. Details of their passages will be found in the appendixes.

The *Plymouth* remained at Honolulu for twenty days. It was later reported in Sydney that on her arrival at the Sandwich Islands she had been sold and her cargo discharged. No confirmation of this report has been found in Hawaiian records, but it may be significant that when she sailed for San Francisco, Captain Gould had been succeeded in command by his first officer, J. F. Church.[4]

The poorest passage was that of the *Lindsays*, an old and not very seaworthy barque. She was ninety-two days reaching Honolulu and when she at last arrived at San Francisco she was thirty-one days out from Honolulu and one hundred and forty-eight from Port Jackson. At one time she must have been a fast sailer, as she was employed in the slave trade. However, she was captured and condemned as a prize in the Vice Court of Admiralty at Bermuda in 1833, and five years later became a Hobart whaler.[5] She was leaky when she reached Honolulu and had to undergo repairs before she was able to resume her voyage.

The ships from 'Down Under' had not been the first to arrive. Many others had preceded them from all parts of the world and considerable quantities of freight already had been landed. Consequently, the Australian speculators did not do as well with their investments as they had expected. A few, no doubt, made handsome profits, but the majority found they had merely lightened their bank accounts. Either they had been forestalled in the market or they had shipped merchandise for which there was no demand.

The *William Hill*, for instance, had much of her cargo still aboard when she sailed from San Francisco about a month later. Every effort to sell it had failed. A considerable portion was landed at Tahiti, probably in exchange for sperm oil and coconut oil, but such items as clothing, woollens, paint, oil, turpentine, saddlery, nails, glass, brandy, rum, wine, tobacco and paint brushes were brought back to Sydney.[6] The *Despatch* also returned to Sydney with some of her original cargo.[7]

The *Lindsays*, which probably had been fortunate to arrive at all, was condemned as unseaworthy and was beached to serve as a storeship.[8] The *Eleanor Lancaster* also became a storeship. After discharging her passengers and cargo she sailed to the mouth of the Sacramento River, thirty-five miles away, and remained there while Captain Lodge ferried passengers up or across the river in the ship's boats. Her crew had deserted, but by paying high wages Lodge secured sufficient men to form a boat's crew. Apparently he entertained miners aboard the *Eleanor Lancaster* on their journey to or from the mines, as reports reached Towns that Lodge kept 'a grog shop and hospital under the same roof'. 'My only pain in your case is, poor Mrs. Lodge,' Towns wrote him. 'Now don't you wish she had a piano? I am aware you are the very fellow to manage the thing if you only know where to stop and say, "Hold, enough." '[9]

After five months at Bernicia, Lodge moved the *Eleanor Lancaster* back to San Francisco. 'I have again brought her to San Francisco,' he told Towns, 'and let her as a bonded storeship till March 1 1850, for seven hundred dollars per month. It is merely the hull of the ship is let, without any part of her furniture, except ground gear . . . Since I have been engaged as a storeship I have had to pay my labourers six dollars per day and three of them do the work of one man.'[10]

The *Louisa's* crew deserted as soon as she dropped anchor. Captain Millton and the supercargo, Eccleston, were forced to discharge the cargo themselves. It was only with the greatest difficulty that Millton obtained a skeleton crew to take the *Louisa* to sea. He had to pay wages of one hundred and fifty dollars a month to secure sufficient men to sail her to Mazatlan to pick up passengers awaiting transport to San Francisco.[11]

The *Eliza* soon returned to Australia, but with her arrival at San Francisco the *Plymouth* sails out of the history of Australia's gold fleet. Her fate is unknown.

After the departure from Australia of the first of the gold fleet vessels, the rush of applicants for Californian passages diminished. Shipowners and their agents sought to whip up enthusiasm and to fill their vessels, but in vain.

The press of Australia strongly opposed emigration to California. The newspaper proprietors, the landowners and many business men feared that any serious drain of manpower would leave the colonies short of labour, with the inevitable result that wages would rise. This they wished to prevent. Later, the belief grew that English and Irish immigrants arriving in Australia at the colonies' expense, under officially sponsored immigration schemes, came out with the intention, not of settling permanently in Australia, but of going on to California. Here again it was the probable effect on the country's low wage structure that prompted the efforts to prevent these immigrants proceeding to San Francisco.

Thus, while reporting the richness of the gold discoveries and the high wages being paid in California, and giving publicity to the propaganda of the shipping interests, the newspapers habitually emphasized the other side of the picture. The lack of housing, the high cost of necessities, the severity of the Californian winter, the danger of illness and disease, the general lawlessness and the frequency of serious crime—all these aspects were brought before the public's notice.

Even the arrival early in March 1849 of the brigs *Spencer* and *Sabine* with the latest news from the goldfields, to which the shipowners gave full publicity, did not bring an immediate rush of passengers.

The 222-ton *Spencer* arrived from Honolulu with three passengers on 11th March. She was in ballast and had come to seek a cargo for California. She brought reports of several vessels having reached Honolulu from San Francisco with large quantities of gold dust, 'which continued to be found in greater quantities than ever'. One man was said to have dug up twelve thousand dollars' worth of gold in six days, three others to have obtained thirty-six pounds' weight of pure gold in a single day. 'The sickly season had set in, causing several deaths,' added the *Herald*, 'and there was a rush to the port to winter, but accommodation was insufficient. Provisions, liquor and clothing were much in demand at San Francisco, but British vessels having foreign produce on board were not allowed to break bulk.'[12]

The 175-ton *Sabine* reached Port Jackson on 12th March, sixty-one days out from San Francisco. Her master, George W. Town, had with difficulty obtained five men at San Francisco to navigate her to Hawaii, having to pay each eighty dollars for the run. At Honolulu he had picked up a crew. The *Sabine's* part owner and supercargo, E. Kingsbury, told Sydneysiders that the claims concerning the wealth of the goldfields were not exaggerated and that each miner averaged two ounces of gold, valued at £6, a day, but he admitted that provisions of all kinds were scarce and consequently dear.[13]

The *Spencer* and *Sabine* took a quantity of varied goods off the market, and on 24th March Broker Harnett reported that but for the extensive shipments to San Francisco the market 'would at the present moment be overstocked and in a most depressed state for many British and other goods'.[14] The passenger traffic was also reviving under the impetus of the news brought by the two brigs. In February only eighteen passengers had sailed for California, and the following month there had not been a single departure. In April, however, fifty-two people left for California. On 25th and 26th April the *Herald* published the official reports of Captain L. J. Folsom, of the United States Army, and these were most imformative concerning the richness of the finds. Any doubts lingering in the minds of Sydney people as to the wealth of the fields were now dispelled.

The revival of interest was marked. More ships were

placed on the berth for San Francisco. Merchants and traders began to advertise goods. Applicants for passages came forward in increasing numbers. On 7th May John MacNamara, exhibiting a flair for salesmanship, erected a tent suitable for California at the Bridge Street end of Macquarie Place. 'Parties proceeding to California will do well to inspect the same,' said his advertisement. 'The tents have India rubber tops and are complete with poles, etc., and can be put up in a few minutes.'[15] Hundreds flocked to see MacNamara's tent.

As one of its readers, hiding his identity behind the pseudonym of 'Cynic', informed the *Herald*, 'a golden field of enterprise had opened up for adventurers' and the migratory spirit had become 'a mania'. 'It would appear, however, that we know enough of California,' he wrote, 'to excite a spirit of enterprise among every class of the community; that the merchant with his wares looks forward to a fourfold return and the poor man, who exhausts his means in the payment of his passage money, sees only before him visions of bags of gold and the perspective of a life of luxury and ease. Whatever may be the under-current, such is the prevailing idea.'[16]

Competition between shipowners was keen, and many inducements were offered to attract passengers. But the cost of the passage was still the decisive factor. From advertisements it may be inferred that there was pricecutting. For example, in requesting passengers by the *Margaret* to pay the balance of their passage money on or before 4th July, Sheppard and Alger stated that after that date the price of an intermediate passage to San Francisco would be raised to £14. The same advertisement gave the cabin fare as £26 5s. and announced that six cabin and thirty intermediate berths were still available. A fortnight later it was stated the *Margaret* had room for thirty steerage and three cabin passengers 'at reduced rates'.[17]

Collecting the balances due from passengers frequently delayed the departure of vessels. The *Volunteer*, for instance, cleared with the Customs on 10th May, when she had sixty passengers. However, she did not sail. On 19th May she again cleared, this time with fifty-five passengers, and when she sailed on 24th May she carried fifty-four. As the number of women and children differed at each clearing and when she sailed, it is evident the composition of her passengers underwent considerable alteration between 10th May and the date of her departure.[18] On the other hand, the *Louisa* between her first and second clearing gained thirty additional passengers in the course of twelve days.[19] Whether this was the result of a last-minute cut in fares, a successful drive to induce passengers to pay up their balances or the transfer of passengers to the *Louisa* from other vessels, it is impossible now to say.

In the first six months of 1849, twenty-five vessels and six hundred and seventy-nine passengers sailed from Australia for California. Fourteen of these vessels and three hundred and ninety-one of the passengers left from Sydney. Eight ships, with seventy-nine passengers, sailed from Hobart, while Adelaide dispatched two ships and forty-eight passengers and from Melbourne there sailed one vessel, the big Dumbarton-built barque *William Watson*, with one hundred and sixty-one passengers aboard.[20]

The *William Watson* was a vessel of 480 tons, well adapted to carry the number of passengers who sailed in her. But conditions in some of the smaller ships must have been shocking. The *Star of China*, a brigantine of only 101 tons, packed aboard no fewer than sixty-five passengers. Built at the Manning River in 1843, apparently by a Sydney shipwright, Robert Howie, the *Star of China* had a length of but 63.8 feet, a beam of 20 feet and a depth of 10.6 feet.[21]

5 *THE STEAMSHIPS THAT DID NOT SAIL*

THE ONLY STEAMSHIP placed on the Californian berth during the gold rush was advertised on 20th July. She was the wooden paddlewheeler *Juno* built at Greenock in 1836 by Robert Duncan and Company. Rigged as a two-mast schooner, she was of 621 tons gross and 362 net. She was 159 feet 8 inches long, with a breadth of 22 feet 8 inches and a depth of 16 feet 8 inches. Her engines, built by Caird and Company, were of 250 horse-power.

Originally the *Juno* had been owned by the St. George Steam Packet Company, a pioneer English steamship venture founded in 1821 by Joseph Robinson Pim. This company ran services around the British coasts, particularly to Ireland. Several of Australia's earliest paddlewheelers, including the *Sophia Jane*, the first steamship in Australia, and the *Seahorse*, which maintained a service of sorts between Port Jackson, Port Phillip and Tasmania, had previously belonged to the St. George Company's numerous fleet.

The *Juno* was owned by the company from the time of her launch until 1841, and during that period was employed on several of their routes. In 1837–8 she relieved on the Bristol–Dublin run and in 1838–9 on the Bristol–Cork route, while between February and October in 1838 she was employed in the company's London services. She had a good turn of speed. On her first trip

47

from Dublin to Bristol, in March 1837, she took twenty-two hours, and later she made passages of sixteen and a half hours from Dublin to Cork and of twenty-two hours from Cork to Kingroad. On 10th February 1838, when rounding Land's End, she found the schooner *Providence*, of Beaumaris, in distress and rescued the five men aboard.[1]

In 1841 the *Juno* came under the notice of Benjamin Boyd. This colourful man, who figures more than once in the present narrative, is best remembered today as the owner of the yacht *Wanderer* and for his whaling establishment on the New South Wales coast at Twofold Bay, which was managed by the marine artist, Oswald Brierley. Boyd was about to leave for Australia to manage the Royal Bank of Australia and to found his whaling establishment and engage in extensive shipping and pastoral undertakings. He purchased the *Juno* and arranged for her dispatch to Australia.

The *Juno* made a leisurely voyage out to Port Jackson under canvas. She left London on 26th June 1841, and anchored at Port Jackson Heads on 25th March 1842, having at the Cape of Good Hope put into Algoa Bay, which she left again on 8th January. Thus she was 272 days out from London and 76 from Algoa Bay when she arrived at Port Jackson. She anchored just inside the heads on the night of her arrival and next afternoon was towed up the harbour. She had four cabin and two steerage passengers.[2]

'Her accommodations below are very superior,' wrote the *Herald*, describing the *Juno* after her arrival; 'she has a splendid saloon, two staterooms and one large gentlemen's cabin, very lofty and roomy, fitted up with fifteen berths, and a ladies' cabin of the same size. On the whole, the *Juno* is the largest and by far the best steamboat that has been sent out to this colony . . . We have not heard of the trade in which the *Juno* is to be employed.'[3]

She may have been the largest and best steamship in

Australian waters, but five years were to elapse before the *Juno* found employment. Throughout that time, a forlorn and ridiculed spectacle, she swung to her anchor in Port Jackson.

Benjamin Boyd reached Sydney in the *Wanderer* on 18th July 1842, almost four months after the *Juno*. Prior to his arrival another of his steamers, the *Seahorse*, had been placed in the Port Phillip trade. However, she had not received the support anticipated and had been run at a loss, with the result that pending Boyd's arrival she had been withdrawn from service. Her owner put the *Seahorse* back into the Port Phillip trade and extended her operations to Tasmania, but if she ever made a profit it was because Boyd freighted her with cattle and sheep for his southern ventures.

Not until 9th January 1847 was the *Juno* registered at Sydney, with George Cowie Forbes, a Sydney master mariner, as her owner. It is not known whether Forbes was Boyd's agent or whether the financial transactions connected with her purchase had not been completed. In May she made a trial trip to Twofold Bay, recording a speed of nine knots, and on 10th June Boyd was registered as her sole owner.[4]

The *Juno* now found lowly employment for a one-time passenger packet. She carried livestock from Twofold Bay to New Zealand. The passage was a stormy one. The *Juno's* rudder carried away and she sustained other damage, so that when she reached Auckland she had to receive a thorough overhaul. On 22nd August she left Auckland on the return passage, but again encountered bad weather, running into a heavy gale off the North Cape. She expended so much fuel in consequence that she had to put into the Bay of Islands to load additional firewood.

There, on 2nd September, Thomas Atherton, her engineer, James Cootham, his assistant, James Anderson, a fireman, with George Church (nicknamed 'The Whisperer') and A. Peckham, two passengers, went ashore in a boat. Presumably having spent the afternoon in a carousal, they pushed off from the shore at dusk, but never reached the *Juno*. Next morning their capsized boat was found and later two oars, two caps and two half-emptied bottles of spirits were washed up on the beach as mute evidence of the tragedy that had occurred. The bodies of Atherton and Peckham drifted ashore eight days later, but those of the other men were never recovered.

Leaving the Bay of Islands on 11th September, the *Juno* steamed round the North Cape. Briefly encountering a favourable wind, her paddle floats were unshipped and she proceeded under canvas, but fierce gales soon struck her and she lay hove-to for three days. On 24th September her floats were again placed in position, steam was raised and she thrashed her way into Port Jackson the following morning with clouds of black smoke spiralling from her tall, thin funnel.[5]

This voyage, which must have involved Boyd in heavy financial loss, showed that the *Juno* was ill-adapted for the trans-Tasman trade, and after another overhaul she was laid on as a regular packet between Sydney and Port Adelaide, calling, when the weather was favourable and sufficient inducement offered, at Boydtown, as Boyd's settlement at Twofold Bay had been named, Port Phillip and Portland Bay. Captain E. J. F. Kirsopp replaced Captain R. Milne, who had been her skipper on the New Zealand voyage, and on 22nd October she sailed for Adelaide, having seventy passengers aboard.

The *Juno* ran to Boydtown in thirty-eight hours, remained there twenty-six hours and then steamed to Melbourne in fifty-five. She was detained at Melbourne for over four and a half days and then called at Belfast and Portland. She steamed from the latter port to Adelaide in fifty-three hours, arriving on 4th November, thirteen days after leaving Sydney. Her actual steaming time on the passage from Sydney to Port Adelaide had been seven days six hours.[6]

On her return passage, the *Juno* left Port Adelaide at

9 p.m. on 12th November and, having called at Portland, Melbourne and Boydtown, reached Sydney at 2 p.m. on 22nd November. During her absence of thirty-one days she had steamed upwards of 2,300 miles in twelve and a half days, thus averaging for the voyage slightly over seven and a half knots.[7] It was a good performance, and the Sydney and Adelaide press acclaimed her feat, but for the *Juno* the Sydney–Adelaide run was not a paying proposition. Her insatiable appetite for fuel, the length of her detentions at her ports of call and the competition of the sailing vessels, which charged lower fares and freights, meant that the *Juno* lost money. She made only a couple of trips early the following year and then, in August 1848, passed from the ownership of Benjamin Boyd, already engulfed in financial difficulties, to that of William Sprott Boyd, who was not related to her former owner.

Sprott Boyd tried to find profitable employment for the *Juno* by seeking a mail subsidy from the South Australian Government and, later, from the Tasmanian Government, but both efforts were unsuccessful. The *Juno*, therefore, was once again laid up. In May 1849 an attempt to sell her at public auction failed, and on 20th July she was placed on the berth for California in a last desperate effort to find her profitable employment.[8]

'No cargo will be taken,' the advertisement announced,[9] 'as the only object in laying the *Juno* on for California is to give those intending to migrate an opportunity of reaching the gold country before the sailing vessels, and all the stowage will be required for coals. Cabin passage, £35; steerage, £15. Scale of provisions and further particulars can be obtained by applying to the commander, E. J. F. Kirsopp, between the hours of ten and four at the office of Messrs. E. W. Layton and Company, Bridge Street.'

Roberts Towns, who at the time was loading the ship *Inchinnan* for California on behalf of Robert Brooks, believed that intending passengers would rush the *Juno*.

'The *Inchinnan*,' he wrote Brooks,[10] 'I don't think can proceed with her California trip. The *Juno*, steamer, has been laid on since, which will doubtless take all the passengers.'

But Captain Kirsopp, daily attending Layton and Company's offices in Bridge Street, found he had little to do. Inquiries for passages were few and there also were few offers of freight. Intending passengers either were not prepared to pay the fares demanded for a steamer passage or, recalling the *Juno's* stormy voyage to and from New Zealand and the long years when she had swung idly at her anchor, were unwilling to risk the long Pacific crossing in a coastal paddlewheeler. Only four days after his first letter to Brooks, Towns informed the London shipowner that, after all, the *Juno* would not be going to San Francisco.[11]

Shiplovers have always regretted that the *Juno* never sailed. Although slightly smaller and with a less powerful engine, she was a comparable vessel to the American river steamboat *Senator*, which made the hazardous seventeen-thousand-mile passage from New York to San Francisco. It would be interesting if today one could compare the performances of these two early steamships in reaching California. The *Senator* and the *Juno*, both sidewheel paddle steamers, compared as follows :

		Built	Tons	Length	Breadth	Depth	Horse-power
Senator	..	1848	754	220·0'	30·0'	12·2'	450
Juno	..	1836	621	159·8'	22·8'	16·8'	250

It will be seen that the *Senator* was the newer, larger and more powerful vessel. Her single beam engine of 450 nominal horse-power had a cylinder diameter of fifty inches, with a stroke of eleven feet. Yet when Lafayette Maynard, a former lieutenant of the United States Navy, placed her on the berth for California, New Yorkers scorned her in much the same manner as a few months later Sydneysiders refused to consider journeying to San

Francisco in the *Juno*. In the end two passengers came forward for the *Senator*, only one of whom, a young lawyer named John Addison, was a paying passenger. The other was Charles Minturn, whose millionaire brother, Edward Minturn, of the New York shipping firm of Grinnell, Minturn and Company, had agreed to finance the venture provided Charles Minturn received the post of agent for the *Senator* on her arrival at San Francisco.

The *Senator* left New York on 10th March 1849. She did not round Cape Horn, but passed through Magellan Straits and, after calling at Valparaiso, reached Panama to find she had been reported lost. At Panama, Minturn had no difficulty in extracting five hundred dollars each from two hundred passengers eager to reach San Francisco, despite the discomforts and miseries they must have expected in so heavily laden a vessel. Against heavy seas and contrary winds, which made the passengers' lives almost unbearable, the *Senator* made a passage of twenty-one days from Panama and reached San Francisco on 27th October.

Her lengthy voyage from New York, thanks to the passengers who came aboard at Panama, had already paid handsomely, and now the *Senator* became the most profitable steam vessel in history. She was employed running to the diggings on the Sacramento River. Although this trip took only eight to ten hours, the *Senator* often grossed fifty thousand dollars on a single passage. The normal fare was thirty-five dollars, with an extra five for a berth and another five for each meal. Her freight rate ranged from forty to eighty dollars a ton. For more than a year, day after day, she carried miners and goods to and from the goldfields, earning in that time more money than any other vessel in the history of either sail or steam.[12]

The *Juno* instead of the *Senator* might well have become the bonanza paddlewheeler of the Sacramento; for had the former Irish packet promptly secured sufficient passengers and sailed from Sydney in the last week of July or the first week of August, she might have narrowly beaten the *Senator* to San Francisco. She would have had to average four knots for the voyage of some seven thousand miles, allowing calls for fuel and using her sails when the wind was favourable, steaming only in calms or against contrary winds. In these circumstances, the *Juno* would have taken about seventy-three days to San Francisco and with luck might even have done much better. Even a seventy-three days' passage would have meant the *Juno* arriving five days ahead of the *Senator*.

As it was, however, the *Juno* remained a 'white elephant'. She was purchased in October 1849 by Henry Moore, a Sydney shipowner and the proprietor of Moore's Wharf, and two years later was sold to the Spanish Government.[13] Most Australian maritime historians have concluded that being 'sold foreign' took the *Juno* out of Australian waters for ever. That is not so; for she came back to Australia to die. In 1853, still flying the Spanish flag and under the command of Jose de Basaguren, the *Juno* reached Melbourne and Sydney from the Philippines. On 20th October she sailed from Sydney for Manila. She ran into strong gales and heavy seas, and on the night of the 22nd sprang a leak. Next day, with the weather worsening, the *Juno* was making about a foot of water an hour. An emergency return to Sydney was ordered, but the *Juno* could make little progress against the raging gale. She strained and laboured in the heavy seas and by 3 a.m. on the 24th the rising waters had extinguished the boiler-room fires. Sail was set and the steamer headed toward the land. Eventually she was beached about a mile to the northward of the Manning River, on the northern coast of New South Wales. The sea at once made a clean breach over her and within two hours she had broken up. Six lives were lost, including that of a woman passenger, but the remainder of those aboard succeeded in scrambling ashore.[14]

And so the *Juno*, which might have been the only steamer to take Forty-Niners from Australia to California, found her final resting-place.

Only one other steamboat finds a niche in the history of Australia's gold fleet for California. When offered at public auction on 11th September 1849, the Sydney-built *Native*, described as a steam packet, was stated to be 'exactly adapted for the Californian trade.' As a further advantage, it was pointed out to potential buyers that her hull might be readily carried on the deck of any of the larger sailing vessels bound for San Francisco and her boiler and engines shipped as cargo.[15]

There is no record, however, that the *Native* either sailed or was shipped to San Francisco, although, curiously, she does not appear to have been registered in Australia. Perhaps she became merely a harbour craft or was converted to a sailing ship and given a new name.

T HE MOST ENTHUSIASTIC of Australia's potential Forty-Niners were penniless desperadoes, convicts or ex-convicts who had been transported from England or Ireland and had known the harsh discipline of the triangles and the lash, and deserters from the army, the navy or the merchant marine. They listened eagerly to the tales of California's golden wealth, endlessly planned and plotted and, for the most part, never left Australia's shores.

But there were the few whose desperate plots succeeded.

On 20th February 1849 the cutter-rigged yacht *Psyche* lay anchored alongside the steamer *Kangaroo* at the Coal Yard Wharf in Hobart. The *Psyche* was of about 12 tons and had been built at Gravelly Beach, Launceston, by the Tasmanian shipbuilder, George Birnie, for James Raven, a Launceston shipowner. Raven, however, sold her to a Launceston resident, W. L. Goodwin, from whom she was purchased, reputedly for £70, by the Bishop of Tasmania, Francis Nixon.[1]

The bishop had the *Psyche* brought round to Hobart, where she received an overhaul that cost, according to a newspaper paragraph, £50.[2] Bishop Nixon placed the *Psyche* in charge of his secretary, George Forster, who transferred the responsibility to his assigned servant, John Hill. The latter slept aboard the little vessel when she was in Hobart and sailed her when she conveyed

The River Yarra, Melbourne, with its shipping, from the south side of Prince's Bridge, by Edmund Thomas. *c.* 1853
(From the copy in the Dixson Library, Sydney)

Hobart Town in 1855, by Kanute Bull, a convict artist (From the copy in the Mitchell Library, Sydney)

Forster to a farm at Three Hut Point or was engaged on some other mission for the bishop.

Hill, a married man with four children, had been sentenced to transportation for life at the Cornwall Assizes on 22nd March 1843, having been convicted of housebreaking and stealing £24. He had one previous conviction, having been sentenced to twelve months' imprisonment for robbing an office. Born near Plymouth, Hill had earned a living as a mariner, a designation which possibly indicated that he possessed an elementary knowledge of navigation and was rather more than a mere sailor. He was physically conspicuous – a very large man, dark-complexioned and black-eyed, remarkable for his bulk, the amount of hair on his body and a scar near his left eye. At the time of his second conviction Hill was thirty-seven years of age.[3]

He was shipped to Australia in the convict transport *Maitland*, which arrived at Norfolk Island on 7th February 1844. There Hill remained until 8th April 1847. He was employed as a coxswain and pilot, and found life so congenial that he asked to be allowed to remain on the island when his period of probation expired. However, his petition was rejected on 28th June 1846, on the ground that it was contrary to regulations. Early the following April he was transferred to Tasmania, but before his departure from Norfolk Island won commendation for good service at a fire at Impression Bay.

In Tasmania, Hill was at first employed in the Government service, working on public buildings as a labourer. On 8th February 1848, however, he was assigned to S. Price, of the schooner *Mary*. In August he applied for a ticket-of-leave, but although his papers were endorsed with a note that he had rendered good service as a pilot in saving the schooner *Waterlily*, his request was refused. His colonial record was good, as the only charge preferred against him had been one of insolence, for which he had been admonished at Launceston in December 1848. Hill was deserving of more sympathetic treatment than he had received, but the convict system was a harsh one. However, on 10th February 1849 he was assigned as a servant to George Forster and a few days later he was recommended for a ticket-of-leave.[4]

On 20th February Hill informed an officer of the Marine Department named Prince that he expected to take Forster to Abbott's farm at Three Hut Point either that evening or early next morning. In the evening Hill rowed over in the *Psyche's* boat to the Government schooner *Swallow*, which was anchored nearby. Communication between vessels was strictly prohibited, but Hill's visit to the *Swallow* was observed only by the convict watchman on duty at the Franklin Wharf and, presumably because he knew what was afoot and had been bribed to remain silent, he said nothing.

During the night the *Psyche* weighed and put to sea, unseen by the Water Police constables or the crew of the guard boat, anchored but forty yards away.

The alarm was given at ten-thirty the following morning. Mr. Gaston, the coxswain of the Marine Department, reported that three of his men had disappeared and that the *Psyche* was missing, while about the same time the chief constable was informed that various articles, including a sextant and some charts, had been stolen from the *Swallow*. Because of Hill's report to Prince the previous day, the *Psyche's* absence would not have aroused suspicion but for the disappearance of the three prisoners assigned to the Marine Department and the theft aboard the *Swallow*. It was quickly ascertained that Hill had not been told to take the yacht to Three Hut Point, while under questioning the hapless Franklin Wharf watchman confessed to having watched the *Psyche's* boat visit the *Swallow*. He was sentenced immediately to three months' hard labour for 'gross neglect of duty'.[5]

It was clear that Hill and the three missing men had stolen the *Psyche*. A search was instituted at once. The

Water Police Magistrate, Michael Innes, signalled the news to Port Arthur, Southport and other stations within sight of the semaphore, and he dispatched the police boat, manned by six constables, to Adventure Bay and the *Swallow*, with a police sergeant and four constables aboard, to Maria Island. But the *Psyche* had a good start and a fair wind, and it soon became clear that she was no longer on the coast.

The schooner *John*, from Launceston, reported having sighted a cutter answering the *Psyche's* description at daylight on the 21st, when, with a westerly wind, she had been headed toward Port Arthur Heads, distant about ten miles, and travelling at an estimated six knots. Another coaster, the *Resolution*, rounding the Pillars at daylight, had seen a vessel resembling the *Psyche* standing out to sea and had reported the sighting later in the day to the commandant at Maria Island. No further reports of the *Psyche* were received and by the 24th it was accepted that she had made for New Zealand.[6]

The men missing with Hill were Rees Griffiths, John King and Matthew Clark.

A married man with seven children, Griffiths had been sentenced to transportation for life at the Glamorgan Assizes in February 1843, for the manslaughter of John Bowling. He was forty-nine years of age and was described as a seaman and washerman. Griffiths arrived at Norfolk Island with Hill in the *Maitland* and was transferred from the island to Tasmania in the same craft. His colonial record was good, as he had not been convicted of any offence since his arrival in Australia.

John King, convicted at the Kent Assizes on 10th March 1845, of burglary and stealing clothes, was sentenced to ten years' transportation. Single, and a seaman by occupation, his real name was John Burrell. The fourth man, Matthew Clark, a married man and a sailor, was sentenced at the Old Bailey in February 1845 to ten years' transportation for inciting persons to commit housebreaking. Clark, who was about thirty-seven when transported, and King, who was the youngest of the quartet by ten years, arrived at Hobart in the transport *Marion* on 16th September 1845. Each had a number of colonial sentences – Clark for absconding, neglect of duty, and feigning illness to avoid work; King for being out after hours and purchasing beer from an unlicensed person, for being found in an overseer's quarters in suspicious circumstances, and for idleness. King had received the heavier sentences. His discovery in the overseer's quarters had brought him a sentence of nine months' imprisonment with hard labour in chains and his removal to the coalmines on Tasman's Peninsula.[7]

For several weeks nothing was seen or heard of the *Psyche* and her crew of four. The authorities and the general public believed that after crossing the Tasman to New Zealand she had headed for California. Indeed, Leslie Norman,[8] citing a letter written by Miss A. L. Chapman, the daughter of the Hon. T. D. Chapman, asserts that the *Psyche* reached San Francisco and was there abandoned by the four prisoners who had stolen her. Later writers[9] have repeated this statement without inquiry, but the facts are very different.

About three months after the *Psyche's* disappearance from Hobart the barque *Freak*, commanded by J. B. Simpson, put into Percy Island, off the Queensland coast below Mackay. There Simpson found two castaways, who claimed to be sailors from the small vessel *Bonna Vista*, which, they said, had been wrecked on a voyage from New Zealand through Torres Strait. Simpson, however, shrewdly concluded that the men were escaped convicts.

He carried them to Escape River, where they were transferred from the *Freak* to the schooner *Coquette*, which sailed for Sydney on 20th May. Simpson warned the *Coquette's* master, George Elliott, that the two men, who had given the names of John Davis and Matthew Clark, were almost certainly runaways. Simpson hazarded the guess that they might be two of the men who had carried off the Bishop of Tasmania's yacht, and he warned Elliott to keep a close watch on them.

The *Coquette* arrived at Port Jackson on 6th July. Through the negligence or connivance of Elliott, the two men were allowed to slip ashore as soon as the schooner had entered the heads. The Water Police Magistrate boarded the *Coquette* as she was working up the harbour, but he was not told about Davis and Clark. However, the news of their presence and escape soon reached him. Davis was quickly captured and lodged in Darlinghurst Jail, where he was identified as the missing John King. However, an intensive search failed to reveal any trace of Clark, and he was never recaptured.

In jail King remained silent about the fate of the *Psyche* and of the other two men, but a report from Captain Simpson disclosed that he had found a skeleton on Percy Island in what appeared to be suspicious circumstances. In a letter to the Colonial Secretary on 13th July, the Principal Superintendent of Convicts said the Water Police Magistrate had advised that a charge of murder was pending against both Davis and Clark. However, in a second letter, written on 31st July, the Principal Superintendent said the charge of murder 'cannot be proved' against King.[10] The precise details have not survived, but evidently there was suspicion but insufficient evidence, and King resolutely refused to say anything that might incriminate him.

On 25th October King left Sydney for Hobart in the brig *Emma*. No charge of murder or cannibalism was brought against him, but he was convicted of absconding and his original sentence was increased by eighteen months.[11]

What happened to the *Psyche*? There seems little doubt that when Hill and his associates sailed her out of Hobart they intended to proceed to California, but through adverse winds or, more probably, faulty navigation they ended up in the Coral Sea. There the *Psyche* was wrecked on Percy Island or some nearby reef. Whether Hill and

Griffiths were drowned in the wreck or in attempting to reach shore or whether they were killed after a quarrel will never be known. It is certain that King and Clark were not marooned on Percy Island by Hill and Griffiths; for if this had happened King certainly would not have kept silent after his recapture.

The seizure of the *Helen*, a regular trader between Sydney and Moreton Bay, was more spectacular, but as ill-fated in its outcome. The *Helen*, launched in 1848, was built at the Bellinger River, N.S.W., by a shipwright named McDonald for Jacob Inder and Company, a firm of Sydney shipowners who operated from the Albion Wharf, Sussex Street. After fitting out at Sydney, the *Helen*, a three-mast schooner, sailed on her maiden voyage to Moreton Bay on 13th October 1848. She was commanded by Captain Chandler, who was superseded the following March by Captain James Wilson. The latter retained command until November 1849, when he was succeeded by Captain George Augustus Griffiths.

At some unknown date after she entered the Moreton Bay trade, the *Helen's* mainmast was removed, its partners and step being left standing, and her rig was converted to that of a brigantine. Despite this change she was still commonly called a schooner. She has generally been described as a vessel of 120 tons, but on dimensions of $71 \cdot 1 \times 17 \cdot 3 \times 7 \cdot 0$ feet she had a registered gross tonnage of 69 1412/3500. The *Helen*, which carried passengers as well as cargo, was thus a much smaller vessel than generally has been claimed.[12]

On the evening of Saturday, 24th November 1849, the *Helen*, under the command of Griffiths, embarked her passengers and moved out into the stream at Port Jackson, ready to sail early the following morning. She was loaded with flour, sugar and timber and carried six passengers – James Wilson, her former master, Henry Austin, John Johnson, Richard Crawley and two sisters, Margaret and Mary Ann Gregory, respectively fifteen and thirteen years of age, who were returning home to Brisbane from school in Sydney. The crew numbered eight – Griffiths, her master, Henry West, the mate, Francis Crepo, the coloured steward, James Painter, the cook, and four seamen, John Roberts, Joseph Lucas, James I. Gregory and Andrew Ramsay. Her complement of passengers and crew thus numbered fourteen; but, unknown to Griffiths, there were also two stowaways aboard—Thomas Ross and John Ryan.

In the morning the wind was favourable and the *Helen* sailed. As she ran northwards along the New South Wales coast that sunny November Sunday, it appeared that this was to be just another uneventful passage to Brisbane. At least, neither Griffiths nor West noticed anything unusual. They did not discover the stowaways, nor did they remark any signs of suppressed excitement among passengers or crew. The events of that evening came to the *Helen's* officers as a surprise.

About eight-thirty Griffiths, sitting on the skylight, was giving West instructions about the logbook when seven men came quietly but alertly aft. Wilson was at their head and all were armed, some with pistols and others with muskets. They moved in a compact body behind Wilson – the passengers Austin and Johnson, the stowaways Ross and Ryan and two seamen, Lucas and Gregory.

'Now, Captain Griffiths,' announced Wilson, 'we are all come aft to commence hostilities. Are you agreeable to our taking charge of the vessel?'

'No, most decidedly not,' replied Griffiths.

Wilson, a pistol in each hand, stepped forward.

'I have taken charge of the vessel to take her where I please,' he said. 'I command you to go forward, sir.'

As Wilson spoke, those with him levelled their weapons at Griffiths. The latter realized that resistance was purposeless, and he was escorted forward to the forepeak.

'Have you any objections?' Wilson demanded of West, as soon as Griffiths went forward.

The mate replied that he had and he also was ordered forward.

A minute or two after West had joined Griffiths in the forepeak two of the seamen, Roberts and Ramsay, and the steward, Crepo, were brought down. Painter, the cook, who bunked in the forepeak, was already there. In the confusion caused by the new arrivals, Griffiths tried to get on deck, but found the hatchway guarded by four men, each armed with a musket. They ordered him below, but Griffiths insisted they fetch Wilson and when the latter came Griffiths asked him to heave to and land them at Broken Bay.

'Go below,' ordered Wilson, 'or I will stop you interfering with what I am doing.'

Griffiths obeyed and the hatches were battened down, while Ryan nailed up the door leading from the forepeak into the hold. Wilson intended to take no chances with his prisoners.

At six o'clock next morning the hatches were removed and Painter was called up to light the galley fire and prepare breakfast. The remaining prisoners were not admitted to the deck until two hours later, when they were given breakfast. The mutineers, all armed, kept a close watch on Griffiths and his companions, but offered them no violence.

After the meal, Wilson summoned Griffiths to the captain's cabin. He told him that he had planned the capture of the *Helen* well before her departure from Sydney. Wilson added that he bore Griffiths no ill-will and promised that so long as he behaved himself no harm would befall him. Griffiths was then ordered to take what he wanted forward, as he would not again be allowed in the cabin. Griffiths, noticing that his desk had been forced open, demanded the ship's papers, but his request was refused and he was ordered back to the forepeak.

'I will land you on the first land I see,' Wilson said, as Griffiths left the cabin.

Ships of the period : the *Phantom*, the *Emma* and the *Chearful* off Port Jackson. From a painting by Joseph Fowles in March 1849 (From the collection of the late Miss Dorothy Rowsell, by courtesy of Mrs. F. G. Marginson, Brisbane)

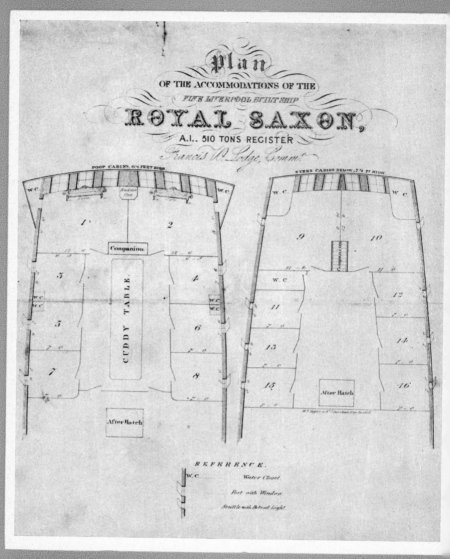

Cabin plan of the *Royal Saxon* (From the copy in the Mitchell Library, Sydney)

On 7th December the west coast of New Zealand was sighted. The mutineers had already considerably altered the *Helen's* appearance. Her white streak had been painted out and the colour of the roundhouse altered from white to black, while the brass plate on the wheel bearing the vessel's name had been removed. However, the *Helen's* disguise was not put to the test, as the vessels sighted were always at a distance.

On the 19th the *Helen* anchored under North Cape. Two days later Griffiths, West, Crepo and the two school-girls were escorted ashore in the ship's boat by Wilson, Austin and Ryan, each of whom was armed with a musket and a brace of pistols. West and Crepo manned the oars. The party landed in a small bay, where the three men and two schoolgirls were left. The mutineers gave them their clothes and a bag of flour and a bag of sugar before returning to the *Helen*. The rest of the passengers and crew had voluntarily joined the mutineers or had been forcibly detained aboard.

Fortunately for Griffiths and his party, the Maoris proved friendly and helpful. They furnished a guide who led West and Crepo to Mangonui, which they reached on Boxing Day. That day the Hobart whaler *Eliza*, commanded by Captain McLeod, stood into the bay on whose shores Griffiths and the two Misses Gregory were camped. McLeod gave Griffiths some provisions and then boarded the brig *Sabine*, which, bound from Sydney to California, had entered the bay and anchored close to the *Eliza*. McLeod informed those aboard the *Sabine* of the *Helen's* capture – an action which was to have serious consequences for the mutineers. Next morning the *Sabine* resumed her passage to San Francisco. At 5 a.m. on the 29th Griffiths and the two schoolgirls boarded the *Eliza* and were taken round to Mangonui.

Fresh-complexioned, blue-eyed James Wilson meanwhile had set the *Helen's* course for California. Reputedly a native of Salem, Massachusetts, Wilson was about twenty-eight years of age and of restless disposition.

65

Originally, he seems to have been a member of the crew of the American brig *Tim Pickering* and then mate successively of the cutter *James and Amelia* on a voyage from Sydney to Tahiti and of the schooner *Castlereagh*, which was wrecked on Sandalwood Island. He next became mate and later master of the barge *Louisa*, owned by Inder and Company, and from her was promoted master of the *Helen*, whose command he relinquished shortly before carrying her off. Wilson, probably because of some physical disability, carried his head a little to one side – a trait which made him easy to identify.

Wilson's chief assistant in the plot to capture the *Helen* was Joseph Lucas, who acted as mate after she was taken. Lucas had reached Australia in the barque *Woodstock* from Manila and had obtained a post as a member of the crew of the coastal schooner *Thistle*, but otherwise nothing is known of him.

Austin, whose real name seems to have been Henry Atkins, was at least ten years older than Wilson and Lucas. He was an infamous character, especially notorious in Auckland, where he had been master of a coastal vessel. Of the two stowaways, round-shouldered Thomas Ross had previously been cook of the *Louisa*, wrecked at the Brunswick River, and Ryan, a carpenter by trade, had served in the Manila trader *Sarah Ann*. Ramsay, a half-caste native of Jamaica, also had served in the *Louisa*, but he and Roberts were apparently detained aboard the *Helen* against their will. Crawley's connection with the sea rested on the fact that he had conducted a sailors' boarding-house in King Street, Sydney. He always denied that he had been privy to the mutiny and claimed that after the event he had been told by Wilson he would have to act as steward. Against this decision, seemingly, he had not protested.

The *Helen* and the *Sabine* both met unfavourable weather after leaving New Zealand. Each made such slow progress that soon water and provisions began to run low. The *Sabine* was carrying forty-five passengers, and her master, George Barmore, decided to bear up for the Navigator Islands to replenish supplies. In the *Helen* Wilson independently reached a similar decision.

On 26th January the *Sabine* was totally wrecked on a reef off Upolu. According to W. T. Pritchard, the son of George Pritchard, the British Consul at Upolu, she was wrecked as she was leaving the island, and he blamed her lax discipline and her 'multiplicity of owners'. Barmore, he claims, was no more than nominal commander. Pritchard was writing many years after the event and as he is not the most reliable historian his account of the *Sabine's* loss must be accepted with some reservations.

'On the day appointed for sailing,' Pritchard says,[13] 'the pilot came on board, but told the captain that the breeze was not strong enough to carry the ship to sea. One owner, a canny Scotsman, said, "Go, we must – we cannot afford to feed all these hungry passengers in port"; another owner, a successful digger, said, "No, wait for a breeze; I guess I can spend another day or two with the kanakas and at the bowling alley", while the captain, a Down-Easter, gave his opinion thus, "——— me, the *Sabine* is a Baltimore clipper and will go where you point her. Up anchor, pilot!" Old Baker, the pilot . . . obeyed orders.'

A boat was sent to tow the ship, but she made little or no progress against the strong swell which often rolls in when there is a dead calm. Baker again advised anchoring, but was again overruled. A second boat was sent to assist the first to tow the *Sabine*, but the brig continued to drift toward the lee reef and soon struck. Her rudder hit the shelving ledge first and she heeled broadside on to the reef, the surf breaching clear over her with a tremendous roar. According to Pritchard, Barmore, standing on the poop by the mainmast, threatened to shoot the first man to leave the vessel before the women and children were rescued. As it turned out, the swell disappeared with the ebbing tide and no difficulty was experienced in saving all aboard. Even part of the cargo was got ashore safely.

Shortly after the *Sabine* had been wrecked a strange sail reached Upolu. She bore the name *Pilot*, but some of the *Sabine's* passengers and crew promptly identified her as the *Helen* and informed Consul Pritchard that she was the pirated Moreton Bay trader. In his book, however, Pritchard's son asserts that 'Sydney' had been erased from the vessel's stern and 'Adelade' painted in its place, and he claims that it was this misspelling of Adelaide that aroused his father's suspicions. If this is correct, it is curious that Pritchard himself makes no mention of the fact in a letter he wrote at the time to the Colonial Secretary at Sydney.

The British Consul's position was difficult. He had no doubt that the *Pilot* was in fact the *Helen*, but without a police or military force of any kind the task of recapturing her and arresting the eleven men aboard was not easy. He turned over the job to his son, according to the latter's reminiscences. Pritchard junior mustered eleven Englishmen and armed them with cutlasses and pistols.

'We launched our two whaleboats, professedly to have a race in the harbour,' he says,[14] 'and stowed our arms under each man's thwart, quite out of sight yet handy when required. Shoving off from the beach at four o'clock in the afternoon, we rowed about the harbour, as if racing and amusing ourselves. At last, running close to the schooner and lying on our oars, I asked Captain Jones [that is, Wilson] if he would allow us to make his vessel our starting-point for a fair race and if he would give the order for the start. He agreed and off we went, but, as previously arranged, made some bungle, which was referred to Captain Jones for arbitration. Again we started, again we bungled, and again referred to Captain Jones. At the third start we pulled the distance and came back to the schooner as near a tie as design could make it, ran alongside and jumped on deck, each man making for the station previously assigned to him, I

68

myself taking Captain Jones. The crew were all on deck – completely thrown off their guard – but seeing each of my men armed, they instantly saw the ruse and rushed for the forecastle, where their arms were piled, loaded and ready for immediate use. Our fellows were too quick for them. Only two of the pirates got below and, slipping on the hatches, they were kept below, as I called to every man to stand just where he was, on pain of being shot. We now had the advantage of having one man more on deck than the pirates. As we ran alongside, my father shoved off from the shore according to arrangement and got on board, just as we had the crew completely in our power.'

There was no jail at Upolu, so the prisoners were released on parole. They made several attempts to escape, but on each occasion were retaken. A makeshift jail was then provided, and in this they were lodged under the care of one Hibbs, who formerly had been a turnkey at the jail in Sydney.

Consul Pritchard now dispatched the *Helen* to Sydney in charge of his son. She carried the passengers and crew of the wrecked *Sabine* as well as Ramsay and Roberts, who had been kept aboard the *Helen* against their will. Since the mutineers were regarded as desperadoes and it was thought they could not be adequately guarded on the passage to Sydney, they were not shipped in the *Helen*, but were detained in the custody of Hibbs to await the arrival of a man-o'-war.

The *Helen* sailed from Upolu on 4th February and reached Port Jackson on 5th April. H.M.S. *Bramble*, tender to H.M.S. *Havannah*, was placed under the command of Lieutenant Walter J. Pollard and dispatched to bring back the mutineers. Constable William Anderson, of the Water Police, having been granted a gratuity of two pounds with which to purchase clothes suitable for the voyage,[15] was loaded with an array of bench warrants for the pirates' arrest and sufficient handcuffs, irons, arms and ammunition to ensure their safe custody.[16]

With the sailing of the *Helen*, the mutineers knew that it was only a matter of time before they would be taken to Sydney for trial. The incentive to attempt another escape was great. Under cover of a heavy gale on 5th April, the very day the *Helen* entered Port Jackson, five of the prisoners escaped after all but murdering Hibbs. They seized a whaleboat and succeeded in reaching one of the other islands. When the *Bramble* reached Upolu, Pritchard believed the men to be on Wallis Island, but they could not be found there. In August the *Bramble* returned to Sydney with only two of the men, Ross and Lucas, in custody. The search for the others had failed.

Lucas and Ross were tried in the Central Criminal Court before the Chief Justice, Sir Alexander Stephen, on 9th October. Both were convicted and each was sentenced to seven years' hard labour on the roads, but the Chief Justice intimated that if they were well behaved their release would be recommended after three years.[17]

From time to time during the months that followed word of the other mutineers reached Sydney. The five men who had escaped in the whaleboat, including Wilson, Austin and Johnson, were reported to have called at Horne Island for water on 5th May, and after one man had been landed at Anatam, the others were said to have sailed for the Fijis. However, on leaving Anatam the boat fell in with the whaler *Brisk*, under the command of Captain Bunker. Wilson and another mutineer shipped in Bunker's vessel as James Parker and John Murray, stipulating that when their time of service expired they should be disembarked at the first civilized landfall. Eventually, they were landed at the Bay of Islands, New Zealand, in January 1851. Captain Bunker subsequently claimed to have warned the local magistrate that he was suspicious of the two men, but no action was taken against them.[18]

No more was heard of Wilson until November 1852. In that month H.M.S. *Calliope*, commanded by Sir J.

Everard Home, called at Rotumah and learnt from an English resident that Wilson had arrived at the island as second mate of the *Pioneer*, of Sydney. After spending three months on Rotumah, Wilson had shipped in the Sydney whaler *Diana* in May as a boat steerer. He was identified by his habit of keeping his head on one side and never looking another man in the face.

The *Calliope* next called at Levuka, where Home was told that two of the *Helen's* pirates were residing on the island of Moala, in the Fijis. At Moala, Sir Everard Home induced the natives to bring in the two men, who proved to be Austin and Johnson. They were taken to Sydney in the warship and stood their trial before Mr. Justice Dickinson on 7th February 1853, but were acquitted and discharged.[19]

No more was ever heard of the other mutineers.

The pirating of the small cutter *William and James* was a miserable failure. She was seized on 12th January 1850 by a seaman named Jefferson and a passenger named Jones. The *William and James* ran between Wellington and Taranaki and a number of ports in the South Island of New Zealand. She was bound for Nelson at the time of her seizure. The pirates placed the vessel's master in a dinghy and cut him adrift, then setting sail for California. However, the captain rowed the dinghy to Queen Charlotte's Sound, where he reached a whaling station managed by a man named Thoms. There he gave the alarm and Thoms at once manned two boats. They gave chase and overtook and recaptured the cutter.

On 2nd March 1850 Jefferson and Jones were charged with piracy before a Court of Vice-Admiralty at Wellington. Their counsel contended that as no proof had been adduced that either the vessel or her cargo was owned by a British subject, the indictment could not be sustained. With this contention the court agreed, and the jury was directed to acquit the prisoners.[20] Thus on a legal technicality the pirates escaped conviction.

7 *THE BANKRUPTS AND THE ABSCONDERS*

IF CALIFORNIAN GOLD drew Australia's desperadoes and ne'er-do-wells as a magnet, it beckoned also those who were in financial difficulties, luring them with a false promise that on the goldfields along the Sacramento they might retrieve their fallen fortunes.

The bankrupts and the absconders were a numerous class. The economic recession had been severe and few had passed through it unscathed. 'This colony is in a shocking state from the low prices of wool,' Captain Towns wrote Captain Goldsmith on 23rd December 1848; 'the amount to refund is very serious – it will require years to bring the settlers sound.'[1]

It was the normal practice for a shipping agent or merchant to advance a woolgrower part of the price he could expect his wool to realize. The amount of the advance was determined by the number of bales shipped through the agent. Interest was charged on the amount of the advance until the wool was sold in England and the agent was paid. Usually the advance was but a fraction of the selling price, so that when the agent received the final account a further payment was due the woolgrower after the advance, interest, freight, insurance, commission and other charges had been deducted.

But in 1848–9 the price of wool fell so low that often the proceeds did not cover the advance. Most settlers, instead of having a credit balance, were called upon suddenly to refund substantial sums to their agents. Moreover, many of them had incurred losses in other directions. The prices of other primary products, notably sperm oil, had also fallen to unprofitable levels, and speculations in the sale of horses in India had turned out badly. Since much of Australia's trade was carried on under an eleborate credit structure, the repercussions were grave and far-reaching. Imprisonment for debt was still legal and with so many traders and settlers either bankrupt or on the verge of bankruptcy debtors found themselves under constant pressure.

This was the primary purpose of the stringent supervision exercised over departing vessels by the Water Police Magistrate and the police. Its main object was to prevent people defrauding their creditors. The protection of passengers by the enforcement of the provisions of the Passengers' Act, so as to prevent overcrowding and to ensure that ample supplies of food and water were carried, and the prevention, particularly in Tasmania, of convicts escaping, were of secondary importance. Each California-bound vessel was obliged to clear with the Customs and the police several days before sailing, and the passenger lists might be inspected at the office of the Water Police. A creditor was thus afforded an opportunity of taking legal action if he found his debtor was about to sail abroad.

The subterfuge of booking a passage under an assumed name was impracticable for many. In such small communities as Sydney, Melbourne, Adelaide and Hobart at this period most businessmen and tradesmen were so well known that they could not readily disguise their identity. Moreover, all who had been prisoners of the Crown – and the police were adept at recognizing ex-convicts – were obliged to produce their identification papers in the form of absolute or conditional pardons or tickets-of-leave, and machinery existed for the speedy investigation of suspicious cases. The records of prisoners were comprehensive and readily accessible. In Tasmania the ex-convict population was supervised even more stringently than in New South Wales, and at Hobart and Launceston the chances of hoodwinking the police were remote.

However, one financier whose imposing schemes had crashed about him in ruin sailed for California without hindrance and in state, leaving behind him debts totalling many thousands of pounds. Benjamin Boyd, owner of the steamers *Juno* and *Seahorse* and the founder of Boydtown, destined in the course of years to become the most familiar ghost town in New South Wales, sailed for San Francisco in his luxuriously appointed yacht *Wanderer*.

Boyd's early history is obscure. He was born in London about 1796 and was educated in Scotland. By 1824 he had established himself as a stockbroker in London. He had some interest in the pioneer St. George Steam Packet Company and acted as broker for this company, presumably in connection with its London activities. In the 1830s Boyd seems to have been in partnership with his brother, Mark, in a broking business, and when he founded the Royal Australian Bank about 1840, the firm of B. and M. Boyd were the brokers for the flotation. The Royal Bank had an initial capital of £200,000, increased later to £340,000. In 1841 Boyd also established the Australian Wool Company, with a capital of £15,000.

Benjamin Boyd came to Australia to manage the Royal Bank and the Australian Wool Company. He sailed from Plymouth in the *Wanderer*, a beautiful yacht of 84 tons that flew the flag of the Royal Yacht Squadron, on 23rd December 1841. The party which accompanied him included another brother, James, and W. O. Brierley, the marine artist better known to fame as Sir Oswald Brierley.

A man of restless energy and vivid imagination, Boyd had resolved to be not only a banker and merchant, but also a whaler, shipowner and woolgrower. When the *Wanderer* arrived at Port Phillip on 14th June 1842, after a passage of 157 days by way of Cape de Verde, St. Helena, Rio de Janeiro and the Cape of Good Hope, three steamers – the *Seahorse*, the *Juno* and the *Cornubia* – and the schooner *Velocity* belonging to Boyd had already reached Sydney.

The Sydney branch of the Royal Bank was opened at 10 Church Hill, where Boyd resided and where the offices of Boyd and Company were also established. Boyd took up large tracts of land in Monaro, Riverina and the western district of New South Wales, and founded Boydtown at Twofold Bay, where he established his main whaling station. He quickly added to his fleet, and by 1844 owned, in addition to the vessels already mentioned, the ship *Terror*, the barques *Fame*, *Juno* and *William*, the brig *Margaret* and the schooner *Edward*. To these he added in 1845 the ships *British Sovereign* and *Lucy Ann*, the barque *Rebecca* and the brig *Portenia*. Boyd disposed of the *British Sovereign* five months after purchasing her, but he did not sell his other vessels until 1848.[2]

To outward appearances Boyd seemed to be highly successful and propsperous, but the truth was that he was financing his ambitious projects from the funds of the Royal Bank, whose directors he misled as to its financial affairs. The end came with the bank's failure in 1849. The shareholders lost their entire capital of £340,000 and, in addition, were compelled to make good a deficiency of £80,000, bringing their total losses to £420,000. Left with the yacht *Wanderer* and a few minor assets, Boyd raised what cash he could lay his hands on and determined to try his luck in California.

The *Wanderer* sailed from Boydtown early in November 1849, and left Auckland, where she called, on 4th December. Boyd voyaged to San Francisco in leisurely style; a correspondent at Tahiti, writing on 27th December, reported the *Wanderer's* arrival there after a passage of eighteen days from Auckland via Tabonia and Matea, and added that she would sail in a few days for the Marquesas, Sandwich Islands and California.[3] Boyd arrived at Honolulu from Tahiti on 26th February 1850, and, sailing for San Francisco on 11th March, reached his destination on 29th March.

Like thousands of others, Benjamin Boyd was disappointed in his expectations of California. He found little gold and in 1851 resolved to return to Sydney. However, before the *Wanderer* sailed Boyd changed his mind and went cruising among the Pacific Islands instead. According to John Webster, who wrote *The Last Cruise of the Wanderer, R.Y.S.* some years after the events related in it, Boyd's object was to 'establish a Papuan republic or confederation.'[4] As Boyd had chartered or purchased the schooner *Ariel*, of 120 tons, as a tender, it is more probable that he had devised a plan for trading among the Pacific Islands or at least of establishing a trading station on one of the islands.

The *Wanderer* sailed from San Francisco early in June 1851, and by the middle of October was off Guadalcanal, in the Solomons. There, on 15th October, Boyd went ashore against the advice of his companions in search of game. Two shots were heard soon after he landed, but except for his belt no trace of Boyd was ever found. The *Wanderer's* crew landed to search for him and as a reprisal for his suspected murder shot a number of natives and burnt down a village. A 'hearsay' version of the tragedy, told to a district officer by a native chief born less than twenty years after the event, ascribed the killing of Boyd to a fear by the natives that he was about to break the taboo on a small river sacred to the natives' ancestral spirits.

After several days spent in a vain search for Boyd, the *Wanderer's* American captain, William Ottiwell, shaped a course for Australia. The *Wanderer* arrived off Port Macquarie on 13th November and was wrecked trying to enter the port next day, stranding on the south shore and there breaking up.

Three years later, in 1854, the cutter *Oberon* returned to Sydney with a report that the name 'Benjamin Boyd' had been found cut into the trunks of a number of trees on Guadalcanal and that natives had reported a tall, long-bearded white man and boy living on the island. These probably were not the first reports to reach Sydney of a mysterious white man living among the natives of the Solomons, and doubtless there were many who thought Boyd still alive. Sufficient funds were raised by a public meeting in Sydney to dispatch the *Oberon* back to the Solomons to investigate these reports, and at the same time suggestions were made that a warship should be sent to search for Boyd.

When the cutter eventually returned to Port Jackson, her master produced a skull which natives had said was Boyd's and which they had given him in return for twenty tomahawks. However, two doctors declared it was not Boyd's skull and the curator of the Australian Museum pronounced it the skull of a native. There was still no proof that Boyd was dead or alive.

Meanwhile, H.M.S. *Herald* had been diverted from New Caledonia to the Solomons. Conflicting stories were told her officers by the natives, but no trace of a white man living on Guadalcanal could be found. The *Herald's* officers located some trees on which Boyd's name had been carved, but concluded that the carving had been done before his death. They decided he had been killed by the natives, who practised cannibalism, and that there was no chance that he was still alive.[6]

Captain Thomas Hovenden's departure for California was more spectacular and dramatic. Little is known of his early history, but in July 1846 he became master and owner of the schooner *Harlequin*, of 62 tons. Two months later he transferred her registry from Sydney to Portland Bay.[7] In September of the following year he became owner of the 83-ton schooner *Minerva*. He sold sixteen shares in this vessel, in July 1848, to John Sargent Turner and thirty-two shares the following January to James Heather Atkinson, thus reducing his own holding to a one-fourth interest.[8] Then, in June 1849, he became owner and master of the *Enchantress*, a brig of 146 tons built on the Williams River by the noted shipbuilder, William Lowe. This vessel was sold to Henry Matthews, of Sydney, the following September.[9] Hovenden then purchased the brig *Lord Hobart*, of 161 tons, which had been built at Salcombe, Devon, as far back as 1805.[10] Before the end of September 1849, he became also the sole owner of the schooner *Will Watch*, of 63 tons.[11]

Hovenden's business premises, which he opened in George Street, Sydney, about March 1849, consisted of an office on the premises of a draper, Thomas James McLelland, and the store which stood next door. He also rented a bedroom in McLelland's house. Hovenden was married to a step-sister of Mrs. McLelland, which facilitated his dealings with the draper. His office was sparsely furnished, but the model of a ship, two globes and a number of pictures gave it a decidedly nautical character.[12]

Captain Hovenden's trade was extensive, but it was not flourishing. In addition to his Sydney business and the ships already mentioned, Hovenden had interests at Portland Bay, in Victoria, where his brother, William, had settled, and elsewhere. He had obtained substantial credit from several merchants, although apparently all his purchases of ships were on a cash basis.

On 3rd October 1849, in that inexplicable way in which bad news quickly spreads, it became known among the mercantile community that in the early hours of the morning Hovenden had unobtrusively left Port Jackson in his schooner, the *Will Watch*. His relatives and friends insisted that he had gone to Portland Bay and Fairy Bay because some remittances had failed to reach him and that he would return to Sydney before the end of the month. However, the prevailing opinion was that he had skipped out of Sydney to avoid his creditors and had taken away with him goods to a considerable value.

The following day, on the petition of Robert Campbell,

senior, and Company, the Supreme Court ordered Hovenden's estate sequestrated. Another Sydney merchant, Alexander Campbell, also lodged an affidavit with the court, stating that Hovenden's counting-house had closed and his clerk been dismissed. He claimed that Hovenden's debts totalled over £14,000, a figure which the *Herald* raised two days later to £16,000. 'How a man in his position could have got credit for so large an amount in about three months is surprising,' the newspaper mildly remarked.[13]

Hovenden had laid his plans carefully but not astutely. Having obtained substantial quantities of goods on credit, he had shipped them to Portland Bay, Melbourne and other places, and had handed a large sum to an employee, George Atkinson, with instructions to proceed to Hobart and there load the brig *Lord Hobart* for California. Atkinson was told to get the ship to sea with the least possible delay. Hovenden then shipped goods valued at about £2,000 for Melbourne in the schooner *Velocity* and put a full cargo aboard the *Will Watch*. On 2nd October McLelland obligingly withdrew £360 for him from the Union Bank, and that evening, leaving his wife with the McLellands, Hovenden made his way to Watson's Bay. There the *Will Watch* was anchored preparatory to sailing next day. In the darkness Hovenden rowed out to her, boarding her some time after midnight.

A favourable breeze was blowing and Hovenden ordered her master, George Merrett, who had assumed command of the schooner on 19th September, to put to sea. At 3.30 a.m., while Sydney slept, the *Will Watch* sailed through Sydney Heads, ostensibly bound for Portland Bay, for which port she had cleared the previous day.[14]

The *Velocity*, with eleven passengers, sailed that afternoon for Melbourne. News of Hovenden's disappearance had already circulated and no sooner had the *Velocity* put to sea than his creditors took action. They dispatched a vessel in pursuit of the schooner and, the wind being light, the *Velocity* was overtaken and brought back to port, dropping anchor that evening in Watson's Bay. She sailed for Melbourne again on the 5th. By then Hovenden's estate had been sequestrated and steps had been taken to recover that portion of the schooner's cargo which had been consigned by him.

A meeting of forty-two of Hovenden's creditors on 4th October placed his affairs in the hands of a committee of five. This committee arranged for one of its members, Alexander Campbell, to proceed overland to Melbourne. There he was to see that the goods in the *Velocity* were seized on her arrival and to endeavour to locate Hovenden and the *Will Watch*.

Unknown to his creditors in Sydney, Hovenden had been forced to seek shelter from the weather at Flinders Island, where the *Favourite* was also sheltering. Hovenden had shipped goods by this vessel also and was disappointed at her slow progress; for he had anticipated that she would already have reached Melbourne and the property been sold. The delay in the *Favourite's* passage caused him to alter his plans.

Some packages which had been shipped for Portland Bay in the *Will Watch* were transferred to the *Favourite*, and the *Will Watch's* destination was altered to Western Port. She arrived there on 14th October. Next morning, anxious to lay his hands on such money as he could collect in Melbourne, Hovenden set out overland on the journey of more than a hundred miles to Port Phillip. He reached Melbourne only to learn that the hunt for him already was in full swing and he returned at once to Western Port, where he arrived on the 19th. Next morning the *Will Watch* sailed.

Meanwhile, Alexander Campbell had received word in Melbourne of the arrival of the *Will Watch* at Western Port. He promptly chartered the steamer *Thames* to proceed in search of the schooner and her owner. A sloop-rigged iron steamer of 88 tons, built on the Thames at Blackwall in 1842, the *Thames* was powered by a single engine of 60 horse-power. She was reputed to have a top speed of nine and a half knots and it was said she was capable of averaging eight and a half knots. The owners of the *Thames* were to be paid £200 for the trip, plus certain incidental expenses. They were to receive double that sum if the *Thames* brought back the *Will Watch* to Melbourne and a further £100 if Hovenden was captured.[15]

With black smoke trailing from her funnel and her eighteen-foot paddlewheels thrashing the water at a rate of slightly less than twenty-eight revolutions a minute, the *Thames* raced at her best speed to Western Port. It was not fast enough. She arrived four hours after the *Will Watch* had put to sea and she could not find the schooner. However, the trip earned her owners £237 17s., which probably was not unwelcome.[16]

From Western Port the *Will Watch* made her way to Jervis Bay, on the New South Wales coast about one hundred miles south of Sydney. There she anchored on 28th October. The yacht *Wanderer*, with Benjamin Boyd aboard, was lying in the bay preparatory to sailing for Boydtown and California, and it is interesting to speculate whether the two men commiserated with each other on their ill fortune or discussed their future plans. Hovenden's object in staying on the New South Wales coast was to meet the *Lord Hobart*, but he dared not remain long in Jervis Bay and on the 30th the *Will Watch* again put out to sea.

As Hovenden had foreseen, news of the *Will Watch's* arrival at Jervis Bay reached Sydney quickly, and the hunt was on again. On 3rd November, after her arrival at Port Jackson that morning from Moreton Bay, the steamer *Eagle*, of 150 tons, was chartered by Hovenden's creditors for £106 to search for the schooner. The *Eagle* looked in at Port Aiken, Botany Bay, Broken Bay and Jervis Bay, and also set a course twenty miles off the land, but without sighting the *Will Watch*. At three o'clock on the afternoon of the 5th the *Eagle* returned to Sydney and Hovenden's creditors learnt that he had once again slipped from their grasp.

On leaving Jervis Bay the *Will Watch* shaped a course direct for California, but when well out to sea Hovenden informed Captain Merrett that as it was on their way they might as well call at Tahiti. There is a strong suspicion that he had arranged a rendezvous with the *Lord Hobart* at Tahiti if they missed each other on the New South Wales coast.

George Atkinson, entrusted with the task of getting the *Lord Hobart* to sea, sailed from Sydney for Hobart in the *Emma*. He spent £600 in repairing the *Lord Hobart* and purchasing a cargo, included in which were thirty wooden houses. But having prepared her for sea Atkinson went to Port Phillip, leaving her master, Captain Tanner, to get the *Lord Hobart* out of port.

She sailed from Hobart on 1st November, carrying five passengers – three adults and two children. The brig was cleared by the port authorities for San Francisco, so it would seem that, although almost a month had elapsed since Hovenden's clandestine departure from Sydney, word of the sequestration of his estate had not yet reached Hobart. However, Tanner was aware that his employer was in financial difficulties, and when he could not find the *Will Watch* off the mainland coast he resolved to take the *Lord Hobart* into Sydney. The passengers and crew objected, fearing they would never reach the goldfields, but Tanner was adamant. On 18th November the *Lord Hobart* reached Sydney. Three of her recalcitrant crew were taken into custody by the Water Police, but Hovenden's many creditors greeted the news of her arrival in port with enthusiasm.[17]

The committee of five decided to sell the brig at once, along with her cargo, making such arrangements afterwards as they could with the captain, passengers and crew. The sale was held by Edward Salamon at his auction rooms in George Street on 23rd November, but although a large crowd attended and the bidding opened at £750, the brig and her cargo fetched only £1,070. Her purchaser, Robert Tooth, placed her on the berth for California, and under the command of George Banks, well known as a whaling skipper, she sailed on 12th December for San Francisco.

By this time the extent of Hovenden's deficiency had been revealed. When all debts had been proved with the official assignee, George King, they were found to total £22,043 3s. 3d. Sydney's leading business men and firms had almost all been caught by Hovenden – thirteen of them for amounts exceeding £500 each. The largest creditor was Thomas Woolley, a merchant and ship-owner, to whom £1,867 7s. 9d. was owing. Others with over £1,000 due included the old-established firm of Robert Campbell senior and Company (£1,261 1s. 8d.), Levicks and Piper (£1,178 19s. 7d.), Smith, Croft and Company (£1,042 9s. 0d.) and the city's largest chemists, Ambrose and Foss (£1,012 1s. 7d.). In the end, Hovenden's creditors received no more than 5s. 6½d. in the pound, and they had to wait until 6th October 1852 for the sixth and final dividend of 3d. in the pound.[18]

Hovenden never reached California. The *Will Watch* arrived at Tahiti on 19th December, the passage from Jervis Bay having occupied fifty days. On his employer's instructions, Merrett sold about a third of the cargo. The demand was good, from twenty-five to thirty-five per cent on invoice value being paid. In all, about a thousand pounds was realized. Influenced perhaps by this excellent profit, Hovenden relinquished his intention of going to California. He sold other portions of the cargo and then disposed of the *Will Watch*.

On 4th April 1850 George Atkinson arrived at Tahiti. His appearance in Tahiti while Hovenden was there can scarcely have been fortuitous, but must have been by arrangement. Atkinson left again on 7th June, when, according to his evidence at a subsequent inquiry into Hovenden's affairs, the captain was still on the island.[19]

Hovenden received a substantial sum of money while at Tahiti and it may not have all come from the sale of the *Will Watch* and her cargo. It is not known when or how he left or where he went from Tahiti. After Atkinson's testimony, Hovenden steps out of the pages of history as abruptly and unobtrusively as he stepped into them.

Another absconder was Francis John King, junior, a Sydney master mariner of whom little is known. He may have been identical with the Francis John King who was appointed master of the brigantine *Faith* on 30th April 1841.[20] Be that as it may, the absconder King some years later chartered the schooner *Matilda* from John Robertson, a Sydney timber merchant. This venture was unsuccessful, and when King sailed for California he owed Robertson £16 13s. 4d. on account of the charter. King's estate had been sequestrated on 22nd December 1843, when the liquidator's statement showed a deficiency of £1,161 9s. When he sailed for California in 1849 King was presumably still an undischarged bankrupt and he left a fresh lot of creditors behind him.[21]

King left Sydney on 27th October in the schooner *Eliza*, of which it was said he was both owner and master, but no proof of his ownership has been found. The *Eliza's* register is not at the Sydney Customs House, but the vessel may have been registered at another port. She was cleared for Newcastle and sailed ostensibly for that port, but a few days later it was reported that 'from what has since transpired there is every reason to imagine that she has proceeded to California and taken several passengers with her'.[22] This conjecture was well grounded. The *Eliza*, a vessel of only 33 tons, took 162 days to cross the Pacific. She arrived at San Francisco on 7th April 1850, and there Francis John King was gathered up among the hundreds of thousands of gold-seekers pouring into the country.

8 JOINT STOCK AND CO-OPERATIVE VENTURES

JOINT STOCK ventures, designed to enable groups of individuals to reach California and undertake mining on a co-operative basis, were everywhere launched when the gold mania was at its height. All over the world such syndicates were formed. Australia provided her share, but they were no more successful than those in other countries.

The earliest attempt to found a co-operative movement for emigration to California was made, strangely enough, in unenthusiastic Melbourne; and this within a few weeks of the published announcement of the discovery of gold. An anonymous advertisement, published in the press and circulated also on placards, summoned those considering emigrating to California to meet at the Commercial Inn, in Collins Street, at eight o'clock on the evening of 18th January 1849, 'to concert measures for procuring the cheapest and most expeditious means of transit to the newly-discovered Gold Mine'.[1]

A 'very numerous' attendance responded. The meeting's chairman was a young mechanic, one McCoy, and after various speeches, a motion was carried appointing Messrs. McCoy, Short and Elford a committee to ascertain at what rates a vessel might be chartered to make the passage from Port Phillip to San Francisco. The meeting then adjourned.[2]

Newspaper accounts of the proceedings are all

unfavourable. 'The room was crowded,' said the *Morning Herald*, 'nine-tenths of the inmates consisting of that portion of the community who are too lazy to work.' From this report it seems that, with one exception, all present 'concurred in believing a trip to California the only thing necessary to make their fortunes'. The exception was Joseph William Hooson, who 'made the most sensible speech, contending that Australia Felix was a far better country for the industrious artisan or labouring man, and adduced a very forcible argumentum ad hominen by comparing the cost of a beef steak in both countries. "A beef steak," says he, "will cost the poor man there two shillings a pound, while here he can get it for twopence." The "sense" or rather non-"sense" of the meeting, however, were opposed to Hooson's homely reasoning . . .'

'No doubt,' added the *Morning Herald*, 'some persons will benefit by this insane speculation : the party who may have stores for sale, and the merchant who may be anxious for the chartering of a spare vessel, will do all they can to promote such a mad chimera. Time will show that they will be the only gainers by this transaction and that the affair will turn out a second edition of the Valparaiso humbug, which unsettled and ruined so many persons here a few years ago.'[3]

The *Daily News* admitted the meeting was 'rather numerously attended', but described it as 'a feeble attempt . . . to extend the California mania which has already created so much sensation in Sydney, to this province, but we were happy to perceive from the reception which the suggestion of a few designing individuals met with to sell all and sail for California, no reasonable apprehensions can be ascertained of any parties being so far deluded as to proceed there except those whose absence would be a blessing'. This newspaper disclosed that 'Mr. Hornblower, late insolvent, was appointed secretary', and that Hooson, whose speech it applauded, was nicknamed 'Old Blatherum'.[4]

At the adjourned meeting on 22nd January it was announced that Captain Petherbridge was willing to place the barque *Thomas Lowry*, a well-known regular trader, on the berth for California if sufficient inducement offered. A clerk from the office of G. S. Brodie, the vessel's agent, confirmed this. Between forty and fifty people were willing to reserve passages immediately.[5]

Those attending the meeting had expected to obtain a passage at from £10 to £13 for an adult and half that fare for a child, but Captain Petherbridge demanded 150 passengers at £15 each and 150 tons of freight at £20 a ton. Unless passengers and freight were forthcoming at these rates, he would not sail for San Francisco.[6] These rates were high, especially that for freight. The fare was £5 higher than the cost of a steerage passage from Sydney, where freight was being booked at £4 or £5 a ton. Had Captain Petherbridge's demands been met, he would have received £5,250 in fares and freight and certainly would have made a large profit.

But the majority of those willing to emigrate lacked the necessary capital and the co-operative movement died quickly. Neither sufficient passengers nor sufficient freight offered, and on 10th February the *Thomas Lowry* sailed in ballast for Hong Kong.

In Sydney the first attempt to found a joint stock expedition was made in June, but its promoter remains anonymous. The advertisement he published, headed 'California', read: 'A gentleman, for many years an officer and commander in the East India maritime service, is desirous of forming an expedition to California; it is his intention to divide the expedition into shares of ten pounds each. No person to invest a larger sum than £100. Passage money, including the profits, to be distributed according to the number of shares held by each member. For further particulars address A. D. California at the *Herald* office, stating names, professions and number of shares required.'[7]

A rival expedition, however, was already in the field

and its existence was at once announced in an advertisement published by William Redman, a solicitor, of 82 Pitt Street, Sydney. It also was headed 'California' and read: 'A party of gentlemen about to proceed to the gold region, having duly weighed all the circumstances connected therewith, and being fully satisfied of the quantity and quality of the precious metal to be procured there, have resolved to organize themselves in a sufficient body for the sake of economy and protection. With this view, they have now chartered a first-rate vessel of 160 tons, whose sailing and weather qualities have been well tested. The party now formed consists of fourteen, independent of the captain and crew, and they deem it desirable to extend the number to twenty; six more are therefore required, and the following are the liberal terms offered them: The sum to be paid is sixty pounds each; for this they enjoy a passage to California, the use of the vessel and everything it contains for seven months (the time for which the vessel is chartered), and a full share of all the gold collected by the party. The sixty pounds entitles each to board, lodging, provisions and the full use and benefit of the ship, boats, and implements, etc., for the seven months, and a passage back to Sydney. Everything necessary is provided in the shape of whaleboats, ammunition, swivel guns, and all other arms necessary for the most careful and efficient protection. The intention is to proceed by water as far as possible to the object in pursuit. The accommodations will be very superior, the cabin being 6ft. 6in. high, and the births [sic] arranged with regard to health, comfort and convenience, this being deemed essentially necessary, as the grand object is to save the enormous expense (but little comfort) of board and lodging on shore.

'There will be room for a few passengers at twenty pounds each, who will find the accommodations far superior to anything offered at the price; *but there will be no steerage passengers taken.*'

It was added that one member of the party was well

acquainted with California and that interested parties should apply personally to Redman, producing satisfactory references if unknown.[8]

Later, additional particulars were given. The vessel chartered was the brigantine *John and Charlotte*, and it was disclosed that a prime mover in the venture was an unnamed surgeon of the Royal Navy. It was stated that the services of the brigantine's owner, Captain Alexander Skene Sturgeon, 'whose urbanity, gentlemanly conduct and skilfulness have been highly spoken of by those who have twice chartered the vessel before', had been engaged. Several people had applied already for the six vacancies. Redman's new advertisement stressed that a director or some other officer would be invested with authority and that other arrangements required to be completed. He called a meeting to discuss these matters and 'to frame a code of regulations to be subsequently confirmed or altered by the whole party'.[9]

At a meeting on 28th June the proposed rules and regulations were unanimously adopted. A further advertisement, signed by Redman as 'solicitor for the company', stated : 'In consequence of the stirring news just received, more than confirming all previous reports as to the superabundance of gold procured in California, it is now contemplated to extend the party, to ensure complete protection and to afford greater facilities to the undertaking, and in consequence also of further rejection of two others by Dr. Reid, of the Royal Navy, who accompanies the expedition as president, a vacancy is now left for a few. The doctor is rather particular in this respect, as one of the rules of the company entitles a member to his full share of gold notwithstanding sickness or death. Amongst the numerous implements for the expedition there is a patent machine provided – the peculiar use of which must be known only to the party but concealed from the public at present.'[10]

Although described by the company as a brigantine, the *John and Charlotte* was officially registered as a schooner of 93 tons new measurement or $100\frac{25}{94}$ tons old measurement. She had been built at the Manning River in 1840 and Captain Sturgeon had purchased her on 13th June 1848. She was scheduled to sail, under the terms of her charter, on 10th July, but the co-operatives had made a bad bargain. When the *John and Charlotte* was hove down it was discovered that she needed to be freshly coppered and otherwise repaired. Consequently her charter was cancelled by mutual consent.

This fact was announced jointly by Redman and Captain Sturgeon on 5th July, the members of the syndicate being advised they had the alternative of obtaining a refund of their contributions in full or of leaving in another vessel that had been engaged and was to sail on 20th July. The name of this vessel was not announced.[11]

There seems little doubt the company had been encountering difficulties, due to dissensions among its members. Some seem to have withdrawn, and as the joint announcement stressed that no additional charge would be imposed for the services of the surgeon who had been engaged to accompany the expedition, it would seem that Dr. Reid was among their number. Moreover, a separate advertisement was signed by William Redman, not as solicitor for the company, but as attorney for the owner of the vessel. This announced that additional members might be accepted into the syndicate and that a few intermediate passengers would be accommodated at £22 10s. each.[12]

This is the last heard of this expedition. Some members of the syndicate or an entirely new group of individuals attempted to form a new co-operative company. Six vacancies were announced in this expedition. The fact that the announcement was addressed to 'respectable persons who are really temperate, active, consistent and persevering, and who are competent and willing to be industrious, as such only will ensure unanimity to all concerned' may have no significance, but it certainly suggests that internal quarrels had caused the disbandment of the previous syndicate.

Applicants, who would be bound strictly by 'certain defined regulations', were offered a cabin passage to California, provisions for twelve months, a liberal share in the profits of the adventure and conveyance back to Sydney. The unnamed vessel was said to be of 93 tons burthen, entirely new, well armed and appropriately equipped. It was added that all her owners were proceeding in her to California. Application to join the expedition had to be made by letter to 'R. H.' at the *Herald* office.[13]

'R. H.' evidently hid the identity of Captain R. H. A. Napper and this advertisement was the first public step in the formation of the ambitious *Sea Gull* venture. An advertisement published almost a month later may also have been connected with this expedition. Its macabre humour makes it worth rescuing from oblivion. Addressed to 'Undertakers – California', it read: 'An eligible opportunity offers itself to a respectable undertaker to proceed to the Gold Regions. A party of gentlemen, leaving for San Francisco, and being anxious to anticipate decent interment, would be happy to give a free passage to any person in the above profession who can produce the usual testimonials. For further information apply to 365 Hunter Street.'[14]

Registered as a schooner but commonly called a brigantine, the *Sea Gull* was a vessel of 62 tons, launched at Ultimo, Sydney, on 19th September 1849. Her builders were Samuel and William Charles, local ship-builders, each of whom retained an eighth interest in her. The remaining forty-eight shares were held by Thomas Smith, of Western Lea, Pyrmont, the head of the firm of Thomas Smith and Company, whose eldest daughter had christened the *Sea Gull*.

The *Sea Gull* was 66 feet long, with a beam of 16.4 feet and a depth of just over 7 feet. A bird figurehead adorned her bow and she was coppered and copper-fastened. 'She has a spacious after cabin, considering the size of the vessel, fitted up with twelve berths.' reported the *Herald*, 'and a fore cabin with a smaller number.' Her master, Richard Henry Alexander Napper, previously had been master of the brig *Alfred*.[15]

According to the *Herald*, a party of about twenty, including her owners, intended to go to California in the *Sea Gull*, remaining away for about eighteen months. Captain Napper was himself a shareholder.[16] Thomas Smith, the principal owner of the schooner, advertised for additional members and circulated a prospectus.

'The prospectus,' stated the *Herald*, 'makes a very pretty statement of the working of their scheme if the profits are, for example, say, £30,000. . . . How these profits are to be made, whether all the members of the company are to proceed to the diggings, or are to turn their attention to mercantile pursuits, is not stated. Suppose, however, that there should be only £300 profit or an actual loss, how are the Sea and other Gulls to get back again to Sydney?'

There were eight foundation members of the expedition – Thomas Smith and his three sons, and George Smith, Captain Napper and the *Sea Gull's* builders, William and Samuel Charles. Sixteen other members were to be recruited from the general public, six of them being full shareholders required to subscribe £100 each and the remaining ten to ship as foremast men, contributing no money but forming the ship's crew. In addition, two aborigines were to accompany the expedition, though for what purpose is not known. The six additional shareholders were to receive four per cent of the net profits – £1,200 each if the estimate of £30,000 profit proved correct – and the ten foremast men two and a half per cent – £750 each on the same assumption. The aborigines were to receive a bonus, the amount not stated. Payments to the six shareholders and ten foremast men would absorb £14,700, to which had to be added the estimated cost of the *Sea Gull*, £1,200, and provisions, £1,000, a total of £16,900.

In the prospectus this amount was deducted from the estimated profit of £30,000, leaving a balance of £13,100 to be divided equally among the eight foundation members, giving each a return of a few shillings over £1,637. If a smaller profit was realized, the members would still receive their four per cent, but 'the shares of the company in that case will be diminished in proportion to those of the members'.[17]

The publicity given to the venture by the *Herald* provoked Thomas Smith and Company to write to the editor claiming that through its 'sarcastic manner' the *Herald* had by no means treated the venture fairly.[18] On 20th November, when the sailing date was tentatively announced as 1st December, it was stated only two vacancies remained.[19] But something now went wrong. On 29th November Thomas Smith and Samuel and William Charles sold out their entire interest in the *Sea Gull*. The new and sole owner was Robert Campbell, tertius, a prominent Sydney merchant.[20]

On 17th December the *Sea Gull* sailed. Her passengers numbered twenty-one, including the two aborigines. Thomas Smith, his three sons, and George Smith were foundation members among the passengers, but Samuel and William Charles did not sail. Five other passengers, apparently, were drawn from two families – G., J. and A. Lumsdale and J. and W. H. Howard.[21] The *Sea Gull* arrived at San Francisco on 1st April 1850, 105 days out from Sydney. If it had remained a co-operative undertaking at the time of sailing, the syndicate seems to have dissolved soon after its arrival. It no longer had any interest in the vessel, which was sold by Campbell's agent before 25th April, and nothing more is heard of it. Thomas Smith and Company's joint stock venture was just one of dozens that at this time started out with high hopes and faded penniless into oblivion.

BY THE MIDDLE of 1849 there was greater aware-
ness of the Gold Country. The news of California's
fabulous fields had spread far beyond Sydney and
its immediate environs and in sparsely-populated country
districts had aroused the same wild enthusiasm. In the
country town of Goulburn, more than one hundred miles
from Sydney, people were winding up their businesses
at the end of June to sail for California,[1] and Towns told
a correspondent that 'one half New England appears on
the move'.[2] Several of the latest emigrants surprised
relatives and friends by their decision to make the
journey.

'You going to California,' wrote Robert Towns to his
brother-in-law, Major D'Arcy Wentworth, who had
retired from the British Army on half-pay in 1843, after
being its first Australian-born commissioned officer, 'and
taking Mrs. Wentworth with you . . . appears to me a
most singular resolution, more particularly at this time
or the time when you will be able to start, say, three or
four months hence.' In a letter to John Pike, Towns
wrote: 'I never feel surprised at D'Arcy's movements,
but I confess this is a staggerer', and he bluntly told W.
C. Wentworth, D'Arcy's elder brother: 'The man is
mad, but he is such a strange fellow I don't like to
interfere with him.'[3]

The truth is that the lure of California was now

94

appealing to the more conservative and stable classes of the community, to those of education or better off financially and socially. 'A great deal of our useful labour is leaving us,' Towns told Captain Lodge, 'much better people and more than we are receiving in exchange.'[4] He told another correspondent: 'People here are all running mad after California – got completely bit by the yellow fever.'[5] The phrase 'We are all California mad' occurs many times in Towns's letters at this time.[6]

Even Towns himself, hard-headed business man though he was, succumbed to the beckoning lure of Californian gold. His roots in Sydney were too deeply sunk for him to emigrate, but he could not resist the opportunity to speculate in ships and goods for San Francisco. 'Most of the people here are California mad, Captain Towns amongst the rest,' Captain H. Pearse, commander of the barque *Inchinnan*, wrote to Robert Brooks in London. 'Having chartered two ships for that port, he was very much averse to the *Inchinnan* going, but the "news direct" has made him alter his views.'[7]

Towns, an astute and careful business man, saw with greater clarity than most of his competitors the probable course of events. From the outset he appreciated that from all parts of the world – and especially from the Atlantic ports of the United States – ships were racing to San Francisco with their holds crammed with goods of every imaginable description. 'I do not attempt to offer advice on the subject,' he wrote, when consulted by Major Wentworth,[8] 'but cannot resist the opportunity of giving my opinion, which is, that the place will be much overstocked with every description of goods, not excepting the necessaries of life. Therefore to ship for that quarter would be madness. I fully expect merchandise of all sorts will be sacrificed for the want of protection, and it will be a first-rate place to purchase British goods at half cost price . . .'

Towns warned J. A. Blyth, who, disappointed at the

returns from his woolgrowing, had consulted the ship-owner about going to California, that 'the adventure is one of great risk and speculation,' and in a letter to Thomas Icely he asserted that 'the adventure is only for the labouring man'. He thought that by the time the ships then loading at Sydney reached San Francisco, all would be over. 'Many articles have sold at enormous prices,' he wrote, 'but the supply will by this time be greater than the demand, as only one vessel had arrived from England and none from the United States . . . The accounts you will see ... with regard to the rate of labour wages is quite correct, but manufactured goods of all kinds may be had for half the price they cost the manu-facturer. What will they be when the fleets arrive which we understand are on the passage?'[9]

Yet despite the caution he enjoined on others, Towns could not resist the temptation to speculate in cargoes for San Francisco. Again and again he gambled in the market by dispatching ships and goods. Of course, he was never sceptical about the extent or richness of the goldfields. 'It's certainly a most wonderful country,' he informed one correspondent, and when Edwin Hickey wrote him concerning the *Chaseley*, which Towns was dispatching to San Francisco, he replied frankly : 'I see many difficulties in the way of your proposal respecting your tenantry and their guarantee in returning by the vessel. Just ask yourself what they would go down for if only for the purpose of taking a look at the land of Dust. No, my dear fellow, their object must be something beyond this, and I would give them very little credit for their nous – like all others, the moment the anchor is gone so are they, whatever may be the pledges and promises beforehand. The fact is I feel much hesitation in giving any opinion on the subject – the whole affair is *wonderful* and at the same time *true*. I have the very best information on the subject, but *dare not* trust my reasoning. The whole affair (to use the hackneyed phrase) beggars all description, a perfect phenomenon.'[10]

Diggers interviewing a ship broker (From a lithograph by S. T. Gill in the possession of Mr. Peter Williams, Melbourne)

Washing for gold with a cradle in California, by W. J. Welch (From the original in the Alexander Turnbull Library, Wellington)

Port Adelaide in 1847, by George Fife Angas (From the copy in the Mitchell Library, Sydney)

The words in italics were heavily underlined by Towns.

On 4th August 1849 the first vessel to complete the return passage from San Francisco reached Port Jackson. The schooner *Despatch* had sailed from San Francisco on 24th May and from Honolulu on 21st June. She brought three passengers, including F. Montefiore and J. C. Catton, and 2,865 ounces of gold dust. Equally important, she brought firsthand news of the richness of the goldfields and a report that Captain Jackson, of the American ship *Inez*, which had left Sydney on 19th February, had refused 4,000 dollars for two horses that had cost him £20 each in Sydney!

In such a small community as Sydney the opinions of individuals counted for much, and both Montefiore and Catton were enthusiastic about the future prospects for both goldmining and trade in California. Their cheerful forecasts caused Sydneysiders to overlook the fact that the *Despatch* had brought back some of her original cargo and to disregard a warning issued by the United States Consul at Sydney, J. H. Williams, as the result of an official circular he had received by the *Despatch*. This circular warned that the revenue and navigation laws of the United States applied to California. Hitherto it had not been possible to enforce them, so that foreign ships had been permitted to enter the coastal trade and foreign cargoes had been allowed to land without payment of duty. But the circular warned that such indulgences might be revoked and a strict adherence to the law enforced, regardless of the inconvenience caused to individuals. It also pointed out that trespassing on the public lands in search of gold was punishable by fine, and that this law would be enforced as soon as the means of enforcement had been created.[11]

The rapidity with which interest in California mounted after the arrival of the *Despatch* may be gleaned from the fact that although on 28th July Towns had been pessimistic about filling the *Inchinnan*, by 8th August he had no doubt he would be able to send her to sea a full ship.

'The *Inchinnan* will now get on for California,' he informed Brooks and Company. 'I have engaged a Mr. Catton, just arrived from California, to return by her . . . Through his information I hope to get the *Inchinnan* filled quickly, but what is to become of her there must be left to chance.'[12]

In addition to dispatching the *Inchinnan*, Towns on 16th August chartered the *Chaseley*, a new ship of 575 tons commanded by Charles P. Aldrich, and, before the month was out, the barque *Duke of Roxburgh*, of 417 tons.

Towns intended the *Chaseley* to take principally a shipment of horses, but under his charter he could ship other goods as well and fill her with cabin, intermediate and steerage passengers. She was to be dispatched direct to San Francisco before 1st October and was to call at only one port en route to replenish her water, if that were necessary. Should she not sail by that date, Towns was to be liable to demurrage at the rate of £8 a day. All livestock shipped in the *Chaseley* was to be wholly at Towns's own risk and the ship was not to be liable in any way for casualties. Towns paid £1,100 for his charter. Of this, £300 was to be paid before she sailed and the balance on delivery of her cargo, but actually Towns paid Aldrich £300 on 1st October and agreed to pay the captain's draft for nearly £725 to another local firm at six months, leaving only a very small balance to be paid on the ship's arrival at San Francisco.[13]

The *Duke of Roxburgh's* master, George P. Collard, drove a harder bargain. He was to receive £1,500 for the entire use of the ship and half this amount was to be paid before sailing. Moreover, Collard was to have the full benefit of half the charter, and as Towns guaranteed that the vessel would make at least £1,500, this meant that as a minimum Collard would receive at least an additional £750. Towns had to find the provisions for the passengers, except that the ship was to furnish water casks and water, and he also had to pay the cost of any alterations or additions to the emigrant fittings, the *Duke*

of Roxburgh having brought immigrants on her last outward passage. Thus, the *Duke of Roxburgh* cost Towns
about double what he had paid for the *Chaseley*.

On 18th August another vessel returned from San
Francisco. This was the *William Hill*, which had left
California on 23rd May. Like the *Despatch*, she returned
with some of her original cargo aboard.[15] The *William
Hill* brought copies of Californian newspapers whose
advertisements indicated that the Californian market, as
the *Herald* pointed out, 'must be overstocked with goods
of all descriptions'. Yet her arrival, like that of the
Despatch a fortnight earlier, gave impetus to the Californian trade. Her four passengers included E. S. and W.
Hill, both of whom not only announced that they were
returning to San Francisco, but painted such a rosy
picture of the prospects in California that they induced
a relative, Richard Hill, to let his house and butcher's
shop at 211 Pitt Street and sail for the Gold Country.[16]

So many vessels were seeking passengers and cargo in
August and September that competition was keener than
ever. Before the end of October thirty-two vessels, totalling
almost 8,400 gross tons, had sailed or been advertised for
San Francisco. The absence of the rates of passage from
the shipowners' advertisements is a clear indication that
price-cutting was occurring. Fares were quoted only for
the brig *Lady Howden* – £25 cabin, £15 intermediate
and £10 10s. steerage.[17] The larger and better-equipped
vessels asked higher fares. The *Inchinnan*, for example,
was fitted up for steerage passengers at £12 10s., 40 intermediate at £20 and 25 cabin at £35.[18]

The general freight rate was £4 per ton, but in some
instances, as for the *Lady Howden*, was reduced to £3.
For horses by the *Chaseley* Towns demanded £30 each,
of which only £4 had to be paid in Sydney before
departure. The balance of £26 was waived if the horse
died on the passage, but if it survived was payable at
San Francisco before delivery was given.[19]

In November Sheppard and Alger announced a 'line

of packets for California' – the first attempt to establish regular communication between Australia and the west coast of the United States. The proprietors of the George Street Packet Office announced that the packets would be dispatched on the first and fifteenth of each month and that each would carry a qualified surgeon.[20] The first vessel, the *Gloucester*, a barque of 297 tons, was to sail on 1st December and was to be followed by the *Harmony* on 15th December and the *Orator* on New Year's Day, 1850.

The line got away to a bad start. The *Gloucester* was over three weeks late in sailing and then met misfortune. She sailed on 23rd December, but sprang a leak when one hundred miles off the coast and on Christmas Day returned to port with her one hundred and fifteen passengers. Her pumps had proved defective and there was a suggestion that her topsides required caulking. This was scarcely a good advertisement for the new line, but repairs were effected promptly and on 28th December the *Gloucester* sailed again.[21]

By early January, within ten or twelve weeks of its formation, the line was in desperate straits. The *Harmony*, although a large number of passengers had booked by her, was detained in port by financial difficulties. John Smith Papps, her master and one of her charterers, had spent all the money he had received for passages and freight and had run up debts totalling £700. He was arrested under a writ of ca sa and placed in the custody of the sheriff, and all negotiations for a settlement with his creditors failed. Meanwhile, the *Harmony's* two hundred passengers had to fend for themselves as best they could, not knowing whether the *Harmony* would sail for San Francisco and with little chance of recovering their fares if she did not. Most had little money and felt they had been grossly swindled of all they possessed.[22]

At the beginning of February, when the passengers, who had expected to sail on 15th December, must have been in despair, Captain Papps called tenders for a bottomry of £800 on his ship. Either this advertisement produced a backer or Papps at last succeeded in effecting an agreement with his creditors. At any rate the *Harmony* was towed to sea at 11 p.m. on 6th February by the Hunter River Steam Navigation Company's steamship *Rose*, an iron paddlewheeler.

The line, however, went out of existence, being unable to weather the unfavourable publicity over the *Harmony*. Besides the *Gloucester* and the *Harmony*, it dispatched only the *Orator* to San Francisco. She sailed on 28th January with one hundred and sixty-eight passengers.[23] Yet though short-lived, Sheppard and Alger's line of packets, with three sailings, had carried no fewer than five hundred passengers for California.

Mining machines and wooden houses were among the most popular items of cargo shipped.

John Austin, who was employed at George Pattrick's steam mill at Chippendale, seems to have been the first to invent a machine 'for washing and separating gold dust from any other sort of soil in which it may be found'. He claimed his machine was portable, weighed only ninety pounds and 'with plenty of water will wash three tons of gold dust in its natural state per day'.[24]

Either Austin sold his invention and sailed for San Francisco, or a rival machine was placed on the market. At all events, Arthur Gravely, whose store was at 320 Pitt Street, advertised that his gold separating machine had been made 'to the order and under the inspection of the inventor, who proceeds with it to California in a few days, and with whom A. G. has completed arrangements for the manufacture of the article, and is now prepared to receive orders'. Gravely claimed his machine was easily worked by two men. The framing was of iron and the machine might be taken to pieces, enabling it to be transported on the backs of mules or by boat; when put together again it could be moved from place to place on its wheels. Gravely, who also sold an 'incomparable cooking apparatus', varying in size from eighteen inches to six feet in length, asserted that his gold-sifting machine quickly repaid its cost by the quantity of work it could handle and the fact that it recovered the finest gold particles.[25]

Wooden houses were always in demand, due to reports of the scarcity of accommodation, the high price of building materials, and the severity of the Californian winter. As early as July a prefabricated house, 'thirty-six feet by twelve feet, well packed and on board, numbered, and plans with it', had been advertised by a passenger who at the last moment was unable to sail on the *Elizabeth Archer*.[26] Presumably this house had been built to its owner's order, but within a few weeks prefabricated houses were being sold especially for the Californian market by William Beaumont, of 221 Castlereagh Street, J. Rossiter, of 250 Pitt Street, Benjamin James, whose place of business was in Parramatta Road opposite the Botany Road, and others.[27] These houses sold well and hardly a ship sailed for San Francisco without a number on board.

What the passengers and cargo aboard a San Francisco-bound ship meant in terms of pounds, shillings and pence may be gleaned from figures for the *Inchinnan*. Towns reported to Brooks and Company that her accounts 'were numerous and heavy', but that she would collect £1,083 9s. 5d. in freight, of which upwards of £850 was payable in California, and £2,894 11s. 8d. in passage money, a total of £3,978 1s. 1d. Towns added that her intermediate and cabin accommodations were not full and that Captain Pearse expected to fill up at Auckland, picking up between £800 and £1,000, 'which will make a splendid freight on the whole in these times'.[28]

If Captain Pearse had obtained the additional passengers and cargo at Auckland, the *Inchinnan* would have grossed around £5,000 for the passage to California, but it appears few passengers and little cargo were forthcoming in New Zealand. The ship's takings, therefore, could not have greatly exceeded £4,000. Unfortunately, there is no way of computing the ship's expenses, so that the profit cannot be ascertained.

A wide variety of goods were advertised for California, but the most curious advertisement associated with the gold rush was inserted by Francis Mitchell, a merchant, shipping agent and shipowner, who resided at Woolloo-mooloo. 'Free passage to California,' this read, 'and a saving of trouble to judge and jury. The undersigned will provide a free passage to California for the thieves who broke into his residence between the hours of one and five o'clock on Saturday morning, upon immediate application and return of the articles stolen.'[29] One wonders whether the thieves had the temerity to come forward and claim the reward!

Outside Sydney, the most active in the Californian trade were the ports of Hobart and Launceston. Tasmania was still a penal settlement to which convicts were being sent from England and Ireland, whereas transportation to New South Wales had ceased almost a decade earlier. The El Dorado across the Pacific beckoned Tasmanians as a promised land – a land where ex-prisoners might find a new and happier life or greater opportunities to indulge their propensities for crime, and where free settlers might rid themselves of the atmosphere of convictism which surrounded them in Tasmania. Melbourne and Adelaide, on the other hand, were free settlements from which all the degradation of convictism was absent.

Even so, Tasmanian activity in the dispatch of vessels to San Francisco was concentrated into the last half of 1849. In the first six months of the year only three vessels sailed for California from Hobart and none from Launceston. A fourth vessel, the *Martha and Elizabeth*, sometimes wrongly called the *Martha and Amelia*, a schooner of 81 tons, is recorded as having sailed for California from Hobart on 17th February, but she did not go to San Francisco. She arrived at Honolulu on 24th June and when she sailed again on 13th July official records show that her destination was Hong Kong.[30]

After May, however, there was no month when a vessel was not dispatched from Hobart, while in August and September there were sailings also from Launceston. Exact statistics of Tasmanian departures for California were not kept by the authorities, except perhaps by the police department, whose records have not survived. The only extant return, in fact, is that of the George Town Police Office, detailing a total of 101 individuals as leaving Launceston for California in 1849.[31] There is little doubt, however, that at least five hundred people left the two Tasmanian ports in that year, more than two-thirds of them in the last five months.

Only two vessels, with 201 passengers, sailed from Melbourne in 1849 and four from Adelaide, one of which called at Hobart in search of additional passengers. The fares from Adelaide were a good deal higher than from Sydney. In April, John Hart, who had gone to sea in 1809 at the age of twelve and had retired in 1846 as a master mariner to embark upon mercantile pursuits in Adelaide,[32] chartered the *Mazeppa*, a ship of 163 tons, to make a voyage to California. He proposed to charge £45 for a cabin, £35 for an intermediate and £20 for a steerage passage and £5 or £6 a ton for freight.[33] The *Mazeppa* sailed early in June, but carried only nineteen passengers.[34]

Although the four vessels which put to sea from Adelaide in 1849 obtained but 121 passengers, interest in the goldfields was more pronounced in the last month of the year than at any other period. Indeed, so great was the enthusiasm in December that more people were contemplating the voyage than had actually set sail from Adelaide during the previous eleven months. The return of a passenger who had sailed in the first vessel dispatched, the *Sophia Margaret*, was responsible. This man, a plasterer named King, told how he had earned at first £19 and later £12 a week, saving £50 in six weeks. Paying £20 for his passage, he had returned to Sydney and then come on to Adelaide to collect his wife, certain

Auckland in 1852 (Lithograph by P. J. Hogan, from the copy in the Alexander Turnbull Library, Wellington)

Mrs. Isobel Fox, and Captain Henry Thomas Fox,
commander of the *Mary Catherine*

that no country offered such favourable prospects for their future home as California.[35] He convinced many others that he was right, and 585 people sailed in four ships from Adelaide for San Francisco in the first three months of 1850.

In New Zealand the Californian trade centred in Auckland for much the same reasons as Sydney had become its headquarters in Australia. The interest of New Zealanders, of course, was additionally stimulated by the number of Australian vessels which called on their passages to San Francisco. They put in to replenish water, to repair damage after a stormy Tasman crossing, to try and fill empty berths or, more rarely, because of the insistence of their passengers, alarmed at conditions of overcrowding or the vessel's unseaworthiness. Whatever the reason, these vessels and their passengers provided tangible proof of the lure of the goldfields.

Disregarding the Australian vessels which called, the pattern of New Zealand sailings resembled that of Hobart, of Melbourne and of Adelaide. The only vessel to sail from Auckland in the first six months of 1849 was the schooner *Deborah*. She was a Sydney craft, but had not originally been destined for San Francisco. Her master, Andrew Bliss, only placed her on the berth for California after she reached Auckland, and when she sailed on 13th March for San Francisco she carried eighteen passengers.

In the absence of official returns, the passenger figures for New Zealand vessels must be accepted with reservation. Neither the central nor provincial officials compiled returns of the number of people emigrating to California. The result is that the figures can be culled only from newspaper reports, and apart from errors due to misprints and inaccuracies on the part of the reporter, the number of steerage passengers was sometimes not recorded at all.

Between March and the end of 1849 twelve other vessels, most of them of small tonnage, sailed from

Auckland and they reputedly carried 183 passengers. The smallest of these vessels, the schooner *Eagle*, of 23 tons, carried no fewer than sixteen passengers, while the schooner, *Vulcan*, of 47 tons, sailed with thirty-five. Conditions aboard these vessels must have been appallingly uncomfortable.

Thus, at least 201 people emigrated to California from Auckland in 1849, and if the figures for steerage passengers are inaccurate, as seems likely, the total may have been much higher. The figures of those picked up by Australian vessels are as difficult to determine, but it is unlikely the total exceeded one hundred.

The few vessels from Australia which called at Wellington provided sufficient berths to accommodate the paying passengers at that port. There is no record of any vessel beginning its passage to California from Wellington in 1849, while the first cargo from that port was shipped in the *Thames*, which did not sail until 19th March 1850.[36] Nor is there any evidence of direct sailings from other New Zealand ports in 1849.

THE VESSELS of the Gold Fleet were a curious mixture of the old and the modern, the well preserved and the decrepit, the large and the small. Big ocean-going merchantmen, vessels which habitually scoured the ports of the world in search of cargoes, medium-sized coasters that plied between Australian ports or crossed the Tasman to New Zealand, and tiny fishing craft – all optimistically undertook the long haul across the Pacific.

Though in the wide sweep of Australia's maritime future their experiences and achievements were to be eclipsed, these ships and their performances will always fascinate the shiplover. Never before or since have so many locally built vessels, constructed of Australian timbers by Australian shipwrights, set forth in so short a space of time on such a long and hazardous voyage. For some, of course, the Pacific crossing proved merely an uneventful passage, but others encountered and overcame dangers, and a few found a watery grave waiting along the way to California.

The smallest vessels to sail in 1849 were the cutters *Phantom* and *Georgiana* and the schooners *Elizabeth* and *Eagle*, the first two from Sydney and the last two from Auckland. The single-decked *Phantom*, of 13 tons, was the smallest. Built at Sydney by Andrew William Reynolds in 1848, she was owned by a Sydney landholder,

George Pike.[1] The *Elizabeth*, the *Eagle* and the *Georgiana*, of 22, 23 and 25 tons respectively, were each almost double the tonnage of the *Phantom*.

The *Georgiana* also was a Sydney-built vessel, launched by an unknown builder in 1840, while the *Elizabeth* was built at Auckland in 1849 by James Gibson. The *Georgiana* resembled the *Phantom* closely, each being square-sterned, with one deck, a single mast, a running bowsprit and no figurehead.[2] At the time she sailed the *Georgiana* was owned by a syndicate, of whom her master, Lawrence Johnson, with a half interest, was the principal owner. Clement Shenly Peat, John White, Robert Berry and Henry Palmer each held an eighth share in her. All four resided in Sydney and were officially described as dealers.[3]

The dimensions of these small craft compared as follows :

	Length	Breadth	Depth
Phantom[4]	34·6'	11·6'	5·0'
Georgiana[5]	40·0'	13·0'	7·4'
Elizabeth[6]	38·0'	13·0'	6·0'

The *Georgiana*, whose single passenger was her part owner, Henry Palmer, made a passage to San Francisco, as detailed in the appendix, of 138 days. The *Phantom*, in ballast, crossed the Pacific in 100 days. George Pike, since she carried neither passengers nor cargo, almost certainly dispatched her to San Francisco as a speculation, intending to sell her, but in June it was reported in Sydney that she had been seized by the customs at San Francisco for a breach of the port regulations. The outcome of her seizure was not reported,[7] but shortly afterwards she was sold.[8] The *Elizabeth*, owned and commanded by William Talbot, made a passage of 100 days from Auckland to San Francisco. The *Eagle*, built at Auckland earlier in the year, was 182 days out from Auckland when she reached San Francisco. Probably she encountered bad weather and she may have been blown off her course, since she called at the Mexican port of San Blas, from where she took 40 days to San Francisco.[9] Reference has been made to the discomfort her sixteen passengers must have suffered through over-crowding and the length of the passage.[10]

In 1850 the smallest vessel to leave Australia was the schooner *Flinders*, of 15 tons, which made a run of 90 days. She called at the Gambier Islands, in the vicinity of Pitcairn Island, and then crossed to San Francisco in 37 days.[11] Many larger vessels made longer passages. For example, the *John Munn*, a barque of 638 tons, which left Sydney the day before the *Flinders*, took 106 days to complete the passage.

Among those vessels whose dates of arrival are recorded, none equalled the *Eleanor Lancaster's* passage of 71 days, but in 1850 her record was both beaten and equalled. The barque *Louisa*, of 307 tons, which had been launched at Calcutta in 1834, recorded 68 days and the ship *Balmoral*, of 357 tons, which had been built at Peterhead in 1848, took 71 days. The barque *Smyrna* may have made the crossing in 70 days, but there is a doubt as to her exact date of arrival. The barque *Thames*, a vessel of 407 tons built at London as early as 1827, made a phenomenal passage of 42 days from Wellington to San Francisco. This was 24 days better than the best passage from Auckland and 26 days better than the next best from Wellington. It seems an incredible performance for a twenty-three-years-old barque such as the *Thames*, but there is no ground to doubt the correctness of her departure and arrival dates and one can only conclude that she experienced a remarkable succession of favourable winds.[12]

The best passages, extracted from the appendixes, may be summarised as follows :

From Sydney

Year	Vessel	Rig	Tons	Days
1850	Louisa	Bk.	307	68
1849	Eleanor Lancaster	Bk.	438	71
1850	Balmoral	S.	357	71

From Sydney

Year	Vessel	Rig	Tons	Days
1849	Gloucester	Bk.	297	72
1849	Inez	S.	356	74
1849	Ebenezer	Sch.	90	75
1850	Crishna	Bk.	271	75
1850	Swallow	Bk.	243	75

From Tasmania

Year	Vessel	Rig	Tons	Days	
1850	Rory O'More			78	From Launceston
1849	Fair Tasmanian	Bk.	155	79	From Hobart
1850	Baretto Junior	Bk.	523	79	From Launceston

From Melbourne

Year	Vessel	Rig	Tons	Days
1849	Union	Sch.	74	81
1849	William Watson	Bk.	480	82

From Adelaide

Year	Vessel	Rig	Tons	Days
1850	Pauline	Bk.	441	83
1849	Joseph Albino	Sch.	142	104

From New Zealand

Year	Vessel	Rig	Tons	Days	
1850	Thames	Bk.	407	42	From Wellington
1859	Saltillo	Bk.	162	66	From Monganui
1850	Orion	S.	534	68	From Wellington
1850	Johnstone	S.	436	72	From Auckland
1850	Inchinnan	Bk.	565	75	From Auckland

There were not many exceptionally long passages. Only fourteen vessels exceeded 140 days on the passage from Australia, and from New Zealand all but three vessels made the passage in better than 140 days.

The slowest passage was that of the *Vulcan*, a schooner of 47 tons built at Auckland in 1849. She was carried completely off course by bad weather and contrary winds, and eventually reached San Francisco by way of Guam, 271 days out from Auckland.[13] Details of the long passages from the appendixes are:

From Sydney

Year	Vessel	Rig	Tons	Days
1849	Petrel	Sch.	69	150
1850	Chaseley	Bk.	516	160
1849	Eliza	Sch.	33	162

From Tasmania

Year	Vessel	Rig	Tons	Days	
1849	Eudora	Bk.	208	148	From Hobart
1850	Augusta	Bk.	372	181	From Hobart

		From Melbourne			
1850	River Chief	Bg.	159	177	

		From Adelaide			
1850	Colonist	Bk.	261	130	
1850	Agincourt	S.	669	131	

		From New Zealand			
1850	Minerva	Bg.	110	140	From Wellington
1849	Eagle	Sch.	23	182	From Auckland
1849	Vulcan	Sch.	47	271	From Auckland

As an indication of the type of craft plying in Australian waters in the middle of the nineteenth century, it is interesting to compare some of the colonial-registered vessels which joined the Gold Fleet. The largest were the brig *Giraffe*, of 260 tons, and the barque *Fame*, of 203 tons, both of which had been built abroad, the former at South Shields in 1834 and the latter at Quebec as early as 1815. The *Fame* was thus thirty-four years old when she went adventuring after Californian gold. Once a whaler belonging to Benjamin Boyd, she was purchased early in August, 1848, by a Sydney merchant, Thomas Winder Campbell. She never returned to Australia from San Francisco.

The *Fame*, however, was not the oldest vessel in the Gold Fleet. The ship *Seringapatam*, which was registered in England, was built at Bombay in 1799 – just fifty years before she sailed from Sydney with Californian gold-seekers. But Indian-built ships, constructed of very durable timbers, were renowned for long life. Even among the colonial-registered vessels there was one ten years older than the *Fame* and another only three years younger. These were Thomas Hovenden's brig *Lord Hobart*, built at Salcombe, Devon, in 1805, and the brig *Bee*, launched at Megavissey, Cornwall, in 1818 and which belonged to the fleet of the Sydney shipowner and merchant, Michael Egan Murnin.

After Hovenden absconded and her captain brought the *Lord Hobart* into Port Jackson, she was sold to the

Sydney brewer, Robert Tooth, who with his brother Edwin ran the firm of R. and E. Tooth. It seems incongruous that a brewing firm should undertake speculations outside liquor in connection with the Californian gold discovery, but it provides a characteristic example of the appeal which the gold mania had for all sections of the community. The Tooths were also owners of the *Giraffe*, whose carved figurehead, as one might expect, depicted the animal for which the ship was named.[14]

Dimensions of some of these colonial-registered vessels, details of whose passages are recorded in the appendixes, were :

Vessel	Rig	Tons	Built at	Year	Dimensions
Regia	Bg.	181	Cochin	1835	80' 9" ×23' 0" ×13' 5"
Star of China	Bgt.	101	Manning R.	1843	63·8×20·0×10·6
Spec	Bg.	168	Cochin	1843	81·0×21·0×12·0
Margaret	Bg.	184	Truro, N.B.	1837	87·4×20·4×13·3
Giraffe	Bg.	260	S. Shields	1834	93' 0" ×25' 6" × 5' 6"*
Coquette	Sch.	72	St. Vincent, N.S.W.	1840	54·0×17·4×9·5
Chearful	Bgt.	124	Leith	1834	70' 0" ×20' 1" ×12' 6"
Ebenezer	Sch.	90	Lake Macquarie	1845	75·3×17·6×7·6
Marian Watson	Sch.	146	Holyhead	1835	72' 9" ×20' 6½" ×12' 2"
Enchantress	Bg.	146	Williams R., N.S.W.	1849	78·5×20·2×11·9
Fame	Bk.	203	Quebec	1815	83' 8" ×23' 8" ×4' 10"
William Hill	Bg.	119	Clarence R.	1847	68·8×17·8×11·5
Petrel	Sch.	69	Port Macquarie	1844	64·1×16·4×8·7
Primus	Ket.	38	Sydney, N.S.W.	1845	49·6×15·1×5·9
Gleaner	Sch.	42	Manning R., N.S.W.	1848	48·8×13·1×7·6
Phantom	Cut.	13	Sydney, N.S.W.	1848	34·6×11·6×5·0
Hyndes	Cut.	34	Sydney, N.S.W.	1832	42' 2" ×15' 6" ×6' 6"
Bee	Bg.	134	Megavissey	1818	70' 3" ×20' 7" ×12' 6"
Lord Hobart	Bg.	161	Salcombe	1805	76·0×21·9×15·3
Sea Gull	Sch.	62	Ultimo, N.S.W.	1849	66·0×16·4×7·1

*Between decks.

Dimensions not shown as feet and inches are in feet and tenths of a foot.

The pattern of sailings altered considerably in 1850. The Californian trade in Australia continued to be centred in Sydney, but sailings from Tasmanian and South Australian ports increased and there was an upsurge of interest in the goldfields among New Zealanders. Sydney dispatched thirty-four vessels for California in the first six months of 1850, but in the same period thirty-five ships left Tasmania – twenty-five from Hobart and ten from Launceston. New Zealand sailings totalled eighteen, while seven vessels left Adelaide and three sailed from Melbourne. In the last six months of the year, however, the sailings were nineteen from Sydney, four from Hobart, two from Launceston, five from New Zealand and none from either Melbourne or Adelaide. The last vessel for California sailed from Melbourne in April, from Adelaide in May, from New Zealand in September, from Hobart in October and from Launceston in November, but in Sydney four vessels were dispatched in November and another four in December.

However, a lucrative coal trade had sprung up with Newcastle, N.S.W., as a result of the Californian gold-fields, and this continued to flourish. The demand for coal, particularly at Panama and San Francisco for the steamers plying between these two ports, was heavy and many sailing ships entered the trade. Loading facilities were primitive and colliers bound for California and Panama had to take their place in a queue with others destined for Shanghai, Singapore, Hong Kong and Lima, often waiting days for their turn. At the end of August 1850, it was stated that the largest fleet of square-rigged vessels ever seen at the port was then gathered at Newcastle, and fourteen of them were waiting to load coal for San Francisco.[15] A few passengers obtained berths on these coal-laden vessels, but their number was not great and the colliers can scarcely be considered as belonging to Australia's Gold Fleet.

Leaving out the Newcastle colliers, the appendixes record the details of 213 passages to California from

Australia and New Zealand in 1849 and 1850, and it is remarkable that of the vessels which made these passages only one went missing. The schooner *I Don't Know*, of 75 tons, built at the Bay of Islands, New Zealand, in 1843, sailed from Hobart on 21st February, 1850, and was never heard of again. One suspects that this vessel received her curious name when her builder or owner first registered her at Russell on 5th May 1843. When the clerk asked her name, the reply must have been, 'I don't know', and so it was with that phrase as a name that she came to be registered. She was owned for a time by the Sydney merchants, John and Robert Campbell, and was then sold to Hobart in 1847. A two-mast, 57-foot schooner, she was commanded on her last voyage by Captain Griffith and carried nine passengers.[16]

Besides the American brig *Sabine*, totally wrecked at Upolu on January 26th 1850, on her second passage to California,[17] several other vessels met disaster between Australia and San Francisco. Having regard to the types of vessel comprising the Gold Fleet, the manner in which they were sent to sea, and the navigational hazards of the Californian run, the number of vessels wrecked, however, was small. Indeed, the Gold Fleet's record, from the point of view of maritime disaster, was surprisingly good.

The schooner *Eagle*, of 92 tons, which left Auckland on 19th March 1850, encountered disaster shortly after sailing. Not long after midnight that night she struck a reef off Cape Colville, having been swept inshore by a strong flood tide. She lost her rudder on the reef, but floated clear. A small bower anchor was dropped, but she began to settle fast and was abandoned, the crew and her three passengers reaching shore in the longboat. The *Eagle* sank that night. Captain John Gray, with his passengers and crew, arrived back in Auckland nine days after they had sailed.[18]

The *Caroline*, a London barque of 330 tons, was wrecked at Honolulu. Leaving Hobart on 6th December

1849, with fifty-two passengers, her passage to Honolulu was protracted. Her provisions began to run low and her water became exhausted, so that she was compelled to put into Kauai Island to replenish it before going on to Oahu. She was 106 days out when she anchored off the entrance to Honolulu on 26th March 1850. A pilot boarded her, but the southerly wind prevented her entering.

In the evening the wind freshened considerably and the *Caroline's* position became perilous. Her cables were slipped, but the attempt to wear and stand out to sea failed. She either struck the leeward reef or was run aground deliberately by the pilot when it became obvious she could not get out to sea. Her main and foremasts went overboard almost immediately, a Finnish sailor being drowned through becoming entangled in the falling rigging, and the ship's surgeon breaking an arm. Many of the passengers, including all the women and children, were taken off in boats from the shore before darkness fell, but thirty persons were still aboard when rescue operations had to be suspended. Next day the high wind and heavy sea prevented their resumption. No fewer than six boats from the shore were stove in during the day and even the largest native canoes found it impossible to get alongside the *Caroline*. Fortunately, the weather abated on the 28th and those still in the ship, which now had seven feet of water in her hold, were brought ashore. Nothing could be done, however, to salve the ship.[19]

Two other vessels were reported at the time as having been wrecked, but whatever mishaps may have overtaken them both reached San Francisco. The first, the schooner *Elizabeth*, does not appear in the shipping lists of sailings, but when she was reported wrecked it was stated that she had left Auckland on 2nd November 1849.[20] She is described as of 40 tons and as being commanded by William Talbot. However, there seems no doubt she is identical with the *Elizabeth* which figures in American records as a schooner of 21 tons and which arrived at San Francisco from Auckland under Captain Kirby on 10th February 1850.[21]

The second vessel was the *Sir John Franklin*. There were two schooners of this name, the one of 21 and the other of 52 tons. The smaller, built at Hobart in 1848, was commanded by Peter Paterson and sailed from Hobart with one passenger on 1st January 1850. She put into Russell, New Zealand, and Honolulu and sailed from the latter port again for San Francisco on 14th May.[22] The other *Sir John Franklin*, which had been built at Port Arthur, Tasmania, in 1838 and which was commanded by J. Church, sailed from Auckland on 11th March 1850, with two passengers.[23] One of these two vessels – it is not clear which – was reported as having been wrecked,[24] but actually both reached San Francisco and, by a strange coincidence, on the same day, 15th June.[25]

The Liverpool ship *Robert Henderson*, which left Adelaide on 16th February 1850, was lost on the return passage to Australia. This fate had nearly overtaken her on the outward passage, as she went ashore on one of the Farallone Islands, a group of rocks off the entrance to San Francisco, during thick fog. However, she was undamaged and was soon got off.[26] After a short stay, the *Robert Henderson* set sail on the homeward passage. However, she got no further than San Francisco Heads. There she missed stays and was driven ashore in a gale. Her passengers and crew were rescued, but the ship became a total wreck and when sold at public auction fetched only 170 dollars.[27]

The barque *Rosetta Joseph* also was lost on the return passage. Built on the Manning River, New South Wales, by Alexander Newton in 1847, she was owned by a Sydney merchant, Moses Joseph, for whose wife or daughter she presumably was named. The *Rosetta Joseph* was of 265 gross tons on dimensions of $88.9 \times 32.2 \times 15.0$ feet.[28]

She left Sydney on 29th May 1850 with eight passengers,

and made a good run to San Francisco of eighty days. When she sailed on the return passage on 15th October she carried thirty-two passengers. During the night of 1st December, when running under easy sail with a favourable wind, she was suddenly found to be surrounded by rocks. A strong current set her on to the north-west side of Clark's or Elizabeth's Reef, to the northward of Lord Howe Island. Next morning her master, Andrew Patrick, decided to abandon her, but the first attempt to launch the boats failed and the jolly-boat was swamped. In the afternoon, however, the wind fell and the sea went down, and by five o'clock passengers and crew were all safely off the vessel. They lay at anchor off the reef all night – twenty-eight in the longboat, fourteen in the pinnace and five in the jolly-boat, a total of forty-seven people, including two women and two children.

On 3rd December the three boats set sail, steering for Lord Howe Island, but next day a gale blew up. In the big seas the boats laboured heavily and shipped much water, rendering continuous bailing necessary. The jolly-boat, which was being towed by the longboat, almost filled, and the longboat had to be lightened by jettisoning all spare clothes, blankets and some parcels of gold dust, so that the five men in the jolly-boat might be taken aboard. At four o'clock, with the gale still raging, the jolly-boat was swamped. The pinnace was then made fast to the stern of the longboat, and by using the swamped jolly-boat as a sea anchor, the other two boats were able to lie to.

The weather moderated on the 5th, and at noon Captain Patrick was able to take an observation. This revealed that the boats, instead of making progress, had been swept back by a strong current to within twenty miles of the wreck. The provisions were running low, for much of the slender supply of bread had been damaged during the gale. As the wind was favourable, Patrick decided to bear away for the coast of Australia instead of for Lord Howe Island, but the breeze did not last.

117

When it ended, passengers and crew took half-hour turns at the oars. Both boats were overcrowded, but the passengers behaved and gave no trouble, except for two or three ex-convicts.

On the 8th, when running before a favourable wind, the boats suddenly encountered a vicious cross sea, due probably to the meeting of two strong currents. The sea washed continually over the boats, which were kept afloat only by constant bailing. So high did the sea run, however, that eventually the boats had to be brought to. A sea anchor was obtained by securing together the masts, spare oars and some canvas, and, when the pinnace had been tied to the longboat's stern, the boats' heads were kept to the sea by using the oars.

About noon on the 9th a barque was sighted four or five miles off, but to the dismay of the shipwrecked mariners their signals of distress went unseen. By three o'clock in the afternoon, however, the wind and sea had fallen sufficiently for sail to be again hoisted. Land was soon sighted, but not until 4 p.m. on the 10th were the boats close enough inshore for it to be seen that a landfall had been made at Port Macquarie, on the New South Wales coast. Patrick's distress signals were noticed, a boat was sent off and by five o'clock the passengers and crew of the *Rosetta Joseph*, destitute and with hardly any of their possessions, were all ashore.[29]

11 *THE PASSENGERS*
AND THEIR EXPERIENCES

AUSTRALIAN CRIMINALS who followed the gold trail to California and there pursued their nefarious activities were commonly branded Sydney Ducks. They were a minority, a troublesome minority, but their brutal deeds were so widely publicized that responsible Australians, with every intention of hard work and endeavour, found themselves shunned and held in contempt on their arrival in California.

'There exists a very strong feeling here against Sydney people, all arriving from the colony being looked upon, generally speaking, as nothing better than convicts,' wrote Thomas Hinigan, former shipping reporter of the *Sydney Morning Herald*, in a letter from San Francisco dated 8th March 1850. 'This may be attributable in some measure to the circumstances of four men from Sydney having within the last three months been convicted of thefts and sentenced to twelve months in the chain gang. Any one who states he comes from Sydney has but little chance of getting on in this city.'[1]

Hinigan had left Sydney in the barque *Maria* on 12th October 1849, and had reached San Francisco by way of Honolulu on 18th January. He thus arrived at a time when the misdeeds of an organized gang of Australian criminals were still fresh in the minds of all. These thieves and bullies were known as the Australian Hounds and were rounded up in the last months of 1849 by San Francisco's irate citizens, who were stirred to take matters into their own hands by the pusillanimous inactivity of the police. No wonder Sydney people were held at the time in anything but esteem!

The Hounds were composed predominantly if not exclusively of Australians, mainly ex-convicts who had been shipped to New South Wales or Tasmania under sentence of transportation. They paraded defiantly through the streets of San Francisco, confident that none would challenge them. Their principal victims were hard-working foreigners, men who determinedly clung to the gold they had earned or mined in the hope that, having accumulated what to them was a fortune, they would be able to return to their homelands. Night after night the Hounds descended on the foreign encampments around the city and mercilessly beat and robbed these men.

The one occasion on which the Hounds committed murder was their undoing. Sam Brannan, the newspaperman, called a mass meeting of his fellow citizens next day and exhorted them to get rid of the Hounds before murder became a regular feature of their activities. The first vigilantes of San Francisco did not trouble to form themselves into an organized committee or to appoint officers, but they acted swiftly. They rounded up the Australians and, for want of an adequate gaol, imprisoned them aboard the U.S.S. *Warren* until they could be given the formality of a trial before a citizens' court. All were convicted and sentenced to banishment, and the determined and aroused citizens then hustled them from the sprawling wood and canvas city.[2]

The Hounds were easily intimidated by an irate citizenry. Indeed, one author describes them as a company of 'young rascals' who paraded the streets under pretence of being 'a society for mutual protection', and who were promptly suppressed when their 'long tolerated disorderly conduct became intolerable'.[3] Very different were the criminals whose deeds caused the formation of the first of the organized Committees of Vigilance. They were hardened offenders, desperadoes who thought nothing of murder. They named their camp on Telegraph Hill at San Francisco, Sydney Town, but they were by no means all Australians. Dissolute Mexicans and ruffians from Europe, England and the eastern states of America joined with the ex-convicts from Australia to hold the law-abiding citizens in the grip of a reign of terror.

These criminals robbed, looted and killed. They bribed police, judges and law officers, with the result that they enjoyed virtual immunity from punishment. Their effrontery knew no bounds, and they held up the rich gambling saloons and committed other crimes in broad daylight. When the police took half-hearted action against them, they were quickly released on bail and eventually were acquitted by bribed juries.

The Vigilance Committee formed in June 1851 found that its first prisoner was a Sydney Duck, actually an ex-convict from Tasmania. John Jenkins was taken into custody by the vigilantes after he had daringly stolen a safe in broad daylight. On the night of 10th June a citizens' jury found him guilty shortly after midnight and two hours later he was hanged on a gallows in the Plaza, where an enormous crowd had been summoned by the ringing of the fire company's bell.

The vigilantes took action also against other criminals. Three, including another Sydney Duck, James Stuart, were executed, this time on a gallows erected at a wharf at the foot of Market Street. All were accorded a formal trial. Twenty-eight others out of ninety-one people taken into custody by the vigilantes' own police were banished. This vigorous action effectively stamped out the crimes of the Sydney Ducks, and few of the later criminals of California hailed from Australia.[4]

In consequence of the notoriety of the Australian Hounds and the Sydney Ducks, it has for too long been assumed that the majority of emigrants from Australia to California were former convicts. Actually, most were free immigrants. As Alexander Berry, a Sydney merchant, wrote at the time : 'I send you a few newspapers by which you will see that there is a considerable intercourse between Sydney and the gold regions, to which, I am sorry to say, many thousands of our scanty population have emigrated in search of gold. In fact, Sydney may be considered as a halfway house between Europe and San Francisco – and I would prefer making the voyage that way via the Cape of Good Hope instead of Cape Horn.'[5]

As early as October 1849, concern was expressed in the Legislative Council of New South Wales at the number of immigrants to Australia who were directly re-emigrating to California, but no action was taken.[6] However, the Agent for Immigration, Francis L. S. Merewether, began compiling statistics on the subject and on 5th June 1850 a return he had prepared was laid before the Council. This showed that no details had been collected of the status of 814 people who had sailed for California from the Sydney district between 16th January and 18th September 1849, but that of the 2,534 individuals who had departed between 19th September 1849 and 6th April 1850, no fewer than 1,455 were free immigrants, 843 of whom had been brought to New South Wales at the public cost and 612 of whom had paid their own fares. Merewether's return[7] dissected the emigrants for California into the following groups :

	Men	Women	Children	Total
Natives of the colony	84	27	283	394
Arrived free at public cost	554	234	55	843
Arrived free at own cost	490	95	27	612
Emancipists	239	17	—	256
Conditionally pardoned	23	—	—	23
Unknown	282	78	46	406*

*Of whom 275 were cabin passengers.

Thus, out of 2,123 adults sailing from Sydney in this period, only 279 were known to have been convicts – roughly, twelve and a half per cent. The percentage for Port Phillip would have been lower still. A return for

Port Phillip submitted with Merewether's figures gave only a grand total of 466 emigrants – 365 men, 52 women and 49 children – who had left for California between 1st January 1849 and 2nd April 1850. Port Phillip was a free settlement to which only a handful of exiles – prisoners who, after serving a period of probation in an English prison, were pardoned on agreeing to voluntary exile to Australia – had been sent, and although some ex-convicts made their way to Melbourne from New South Wales and Tasmania, their number before the discovery of gold in Victoria was not large.

The exodus to California from Tasmania aroused little apprehension, since the provision of cheap labour was adequately assured by the number of convicts already transported and those who were still arriving. Questions were not asked and statistics were not kept. We know only that in 1849 a total of 763 people left for 'other places', a designation which embraced all places except Port Phillip, Sydney and Adelaide, and of this total, 602 ranked as free, 108 as free by servitude and 53 held conditional pardons.[8] Even if California was the destination of all the ex-convicts who sailed from Tasmania, they would still have totalled no more than 161.

Again, a return of outward bound vessels kept at the George Town police office shows that in nineteen California-bound vessels from Launceston between August 1849 and May 1851, a total of 374 passengers sailed. Of these, 208 ranked as free, 57 were native born, 16 were not specified and there were 5 children. The convict element comprised 61 free by servitude and 27 conditionally pardoned, a total of 88 people. This represents slightly less than twenty-four per cent.[9]

The only protection afforded emigrants against unscrupulous shipowners and agents was provided by the Passengers' Act and the supervision of the Water Police Magistrates. Some measure of control over excessive overcrowding and the employment of unseaworthy vessels was thus provided, but the views held in the middle of the nineteenth century as to what constituted ship-board overcrowding and unseaworthiness were vastly different to those now prevailing. As a matter of course, passengers and seamen accepted conditions and standards which would not now be tolerated.

The Passengers' Act computed the length of the passage from one port to another and obliged shipowners to carry sufficient provisions to last the number of people aboard for that number of days. The Act also prescribed the medicines and medical comforts to be carried.

At the time of Marshall's discovery sixty days was laid down as the length of the passage from New South Wales to the west coast of America north of the equator. This was quite inadequate, as is obvious when we recall that the shortest passage from Australia to San Francisco of any vessel in the Gold Fleet was sixty-eight days. The passages of the Gold Fleet vessels which sailed in the first part of 1849 showed the fallacy of sixty days as the length of the passage and on 11th September 1849, it was increased to ninety days. At the same time twenty days was fixed as the time for the passage to New Zealand, fifty to Tahiti or Tonga, and seventy to Hawaii or the west coast of America south of the equator.

To prevent overcrowding, the Passengers' Act decreed that only three souls should be carried for every five tons register, captain and crew included. It was on the basis of this limitation and the prescribed length of the passage that provisions were calculated.

There were many ways in which the regulations might be circumvented, particularly as the supervision of the authorities was never stringent. Inferior provisions were sometimes shipped, announced scales of diet were not adhered to once a vessel was at sea, or a captain might clear for an intermediate port at which he had no intention of calling, this enabling him to sail with a smaller quantity of provisions than he should have been carrying.

Information regarding the scale of rations is meagre, as none of the scales exhibited at agents' offices for inspection seem to have survived. These dietary scales were seldom advertised, but when the *Balmoral* was placed on the berth the scale of weekly rations in the steerage was announced as 7 lb. bread, 2 lb. fresh mutton or pork, 4 lb. beef, 1 lb. pork, 2 lb. fine flour, 8 oz. raisins, 4 oz. suet, ½ pint pease, ½ lb. rice, ¼ lb. tea or 10 oz. coffee, 2 lb. sugar, ¼ pint of vinegar, ¼ pint of lime juice, seven glasses of spirits, ½ oz. mustard, ¼ oz. pepper, 21 quarts of water and plenty of salt. Children under twelve years of age received half the above amounts.[10]

It was also stated that the *Balmoral* would carry, as medical comforts, 50 doz. bottled ale and porter, 50 doz. wines, port and sherry, 20 gallons brandy, 20 gallons rum, 500 pints lime juice, 20 gallons vinegar, 5 gallons chloride zinc, 56 lb. chloride lime, 200 lb. oatmeal, 50 lb. arrowroot, 200 lb. barley, 150 lb. sago, 200 lb. preserved meats, 1,000 lb. fresh meats, 600 lb. sugar and 200 lb. marine soap.[11]

The rations and medical comforts were similar to those carried in the emigrant ships to Australia. The rations, if adequate, were scarcely suited to the warm latitudes of the Pacific or to the needs of children, and they lacked variety, the food being monotonous and unappetizing. The emigrants cooked their own meals if they were travelling intermediate or steerage, except perhaps in some of the smaller vessels carrying only a few passengers. No doubt they formed themselves into small messes of six or eight persons and pooled their rations, taking it in turn to prepare the food, do the cooking and perform the mess chores.

The Water Police Magistrate's supervision, in respect of overcrowding and provisioning, was sometimes lax or ineffective. Thus, the schooner *Petrel* had to call at Monganui, New Zealand, to drop some of her passengers because of overcrowding,[12] and when the *Maria* was advertised it was claimed that 'the system of packing human beings six in a berth like a slave ship will be avoided', which suggests overcrowding was a notorious[13] evil. Again, the brigantine *Chearful*, of 124 tons, embarked no fewer than eighty–six passengers, of whom eleven were women and two children. This was probably about twenty more than she was permitted to carry under the provisions of the Passengers' Act. Not only was she shockingly overcrowded, but her supply of provisions was inadequate, and when she reached Tahiti her pantry was absolutely bare. Her owner and master, Robert Edwin Ogilby, who had been compelled to raise two mortgages on her, one of which was for £500 at eight per cent interest, before he could dispatch her from Sydney, had now to arrange a bottomry bond for £300 in order to replenish her provisions. The *Chearful*, whose name the newspapers of the day invariably spelt *Cheerful*, although her register gives *Chearful*, and which was usually called a schooner, although her register and the Harbour-master's Records at Honolulu agree in calling her a brigantine, was 148 days out from Sydney when she arrived at San Francisco. The passengers by this Leith-built vessel must have been glad to get ashore after having been cooped up aboard so small a vessel for so long.[14]

The combination of overcrowding and inadequate provisions imposed great distress and hardship. When C. S. Deacon chartered the big English ship *Victoria*, he sold berths by visiting Parramatta and other centres to paint a rosy picture of conditions in California, from where he had just returned.[15] The *Victoria's* accommodations were stated to be 'far superior to any vessel at the berth', and passengers were promised that 'a liberal scale of the best provisions will be handed to each person engaging and the same guaranteed'.[16]

One passenger, a mail-coach proprietor named L. Alexander, however, wrote to the *Herald*, complaining in 'the most bitter terms of the conduct of the charterers or owners'. He asserted the passengers were 'stowed away worse than African slaves on the coast of Guinea, that there is no hospital, and that the provisions are shamefully bad, particularly the beef'. So serious were

Alexander's charges that, for fear of libel, the *Herald* declined to publish his letter in full, but the newspaper did point out that before the *Victoria* had been permitted to proceed to sea, portion of her deck cargo had been removed by order of the Water Police Magistrate.[17] The charges were denied by Deacon and the ship's agents, Thornton and Church, and a long controversy ensued.[18]

However, other passengers supported Alexander and it certainly seems that the provisions were of 'the most wretched description' and so inadequate that a month before arriving at Honolulu short rations were being served.[19] A petition signed by 110 male passengers was stated to have been forwarded from Honolulu to the Legislative Council of New South Wales, setting forth 'the scarcity and inferiority of provisions, the want of water, the absence of a hospital and other breaches of contract'.[20]

Besides overcrowding and inferior or inadequate provisions, there were also other directions in which the authorities were unable to adequately protect passengers. Thus, when it seemed that the *Harmony* might never sail because of financial difficulties, it was discovered that the authorities were powerless to take action. They could not order fares to be refunded and passengers compensated for their losses, since the Passengers' Act was not applicable to colonial voyages.[21]

Overloaded and unseaworthy vessels sometimes passed official inspection and were permitted to sail. Thus, the brig *Wigeon*, according to one of her forty-eight passengers, Johnson Dean, who many years later wrote an account of his experiences,[22] was badly overloaded when she left Hobart on 26th April 1850, and was in such a state of disrepair as to be almost unseaworthy. This vessel of 280 tons, commanded by J. J. Capes, was described by Dean as 'in a disgracefully overloaded condition, quantities of timber, horses, hay, casks of water, salt beef, etc., being stowed on deck till there was scarcely room to go fore and aft'.[23]

127

As the coastline of Tasmania faded from sight in the dusk of evening, the passengers sang 'Isle of Beauty, fare thee well'. The wind steadily increased in violence during the night, shortly blowing at gale strength. The single men, numbering about a dozen of her passengers, were located in a deckhouse, and here Dean and his companions lay in their bunks, listening fearfully to the howl of the wind, the pattering feet of the sailors and the shouted orders of master and mates as sail was shortened. About midnight, to the accompaniment of a handspike being thumped loudly on the deck, there came the cry of 'All hands on deck to reef topsails!'

Shortly afterwards the second mate entered the deckhouse and asked the passengers there to man the pumps. His request was refused, on the ground that 'those should work the ship who were paid for it'. At daylight, the request was repeated by the first mate. He was more emphatic, and bluntly told the deckhouse passengers that unless they were willing to assist, all would soon go to the bottom together. So the passengers turned out on deck and, two at a time, manned each of the old-fashioned hand pumps. The hatches had been battened down, so that the passengers berthed below were imprisoned in the stifling darkness of the 'tween-decks.

The water gained slightly on the pumps, and the wind tore sails loose from the gaskets and ripped the jib-boom and other spars from the labouring ship. On the second day, when an attempt was made to heave to, the *Wigeon* went right over on her beam ends and was only righted by the cutting away of the mainmast. Dean says that as the mast went overboard it was checked by a rope fast aloft, and the butt end came inboard again, sliding along the lee rail as it went by the board and almost taking the corner of the deckhouse with it. A heavy sea broke over Dean and his companion at the pump. Dean was carried by the sea along the deck, but was saved by the action of two seamen, who seized him.

The weather did not moderate until the fourth day. A

jury mast was then rigged and the *Wigeon* headed for Port Jackson. Her steering-gear carried away, but was repaired, and on 12th May the dismasted and battered brig reached Sydney.[24] About fifty tons of cargo had been jettisoned and two horses, twelve sheep and other live-stock drowned.[25]

On the other hand, the Water Police in some instances took effective action. Captain Browne, the Water Police Magistrate for Sydney, for example, prevented the 15-ton ketch *Curlew* from clandestinely setting out for California. A woman who had paid £10 for a passage to California called on the Water Police to inquire the vessel's whereabouts in the harbour. This was the first the police knew of the ketch being bound for San Francisco, as when she had cleared a few days earlier her destination had been given as Shellharbour, on the New South Wales coast. Captain Browne boarded her in Woolloomooloo Bay and found she had been fitting out for a long voyage. She had six berths aft and three forward, and there was a large supply of provisions and water aboard. Seized by the authorities, the *Curlew* was brought into Sydney Cove. However, she was released a few days later and then sailed for Shellharbour.[26]

Again, early in 1850, Captain Browne learned that the *Johnson*, a vessel which, he judged, could carry from 180 to 200 people, proposed to embark gold-seekers at Moreton Bay. Browne promptly reported the matter to the Government Emigration Officer, stating that while he had no official notice from the master or charterers, and no advertisement had been published in the press, the facts 'are correct'. If the *Johnson* sailed from Moreton Bay she would not be subject to any official inspection, as there was no Emigration Officer at Brisbane. Captain Browne urged that one should be appointed, and this was done.[27]

It must not be imagined, however, that conditions were unsatisfactory aboard all vessels. They were reasonable in many, as is shown by William Shaw's account of his passage from Adelaide to San Francisco in the *Mazeppa*, which he described as a 'small clipper-built ship of one hundred and seventy tons register'.[28] She had been trading to Singapore and was manned by a Malay crew numbering seventeen. There were five cabin and sixteen steerage passengers, the latter being packed into a space sixteen feet square and four feet ten inches high. But the scale of provisions was exceedingly liberal, 'far superior', says Shaw, who previously had emigrated to South Australia from England, 'to any given out of English ports'. No shipboard regulations were imposed on the passengers, and the greatest good feeling and harmony prevailed on board. While the *Mazeppa* was in the tropics, however, cockroaches and vermin swarmed everywhere and the passengers suffered much discomfort in their confined quarters. 'The ship had formerly been sugar laden,' explained Shaw, 'which accounted for the quantities of cockroaches . . . rats bit us in our sleep.'

In want of water on arrival at the American coast, the *Mazeppa* put into San Diego. There many additional passengers, some of whom had travelled over the Rocky Mountains and others through Central America, were crowded aboard. She reached San Francisco on 14th October, 128 days out from Adelaide.

For most of the gold-seekers from Australia and New Zealand, arrival in California brought disillusionment. The conditions were vastly different from what they had expected. Accommodation was scarce and consequently very expensive, as, indeed, were all necessities. It was difficult to get to the goldfields and even harder to find a place on which to peg out a claim. Employment was not nearly as easy to obtain as it had been originally, particularly in the wet season, when the weather was atrocious and sickness common. Gambling and drinking saloons abounded to ensnare the unwary and the weak, and for every migrant who made a fortune or simply a comfortable living, there were hundreds who found themselves worse off in golden California than they had been in Australia. Long before the end of 1850 scores of Australians were seeking an opportunity to work their passage home or were thankful at having enough dollars to buy a return steerage ticket. Yet there were, of course, some who prospered, making a fortune at the mines, founding a successful business or establishing themselves on the land.

Letters home to relatives and friends, and the accounts of those who wrote of their adventures, reflect the experiences common to all emigrants from Australia and New Zealand. Coming in from the sea, after the long Pacific crossing, their first view of San Francisco was that described by Johnson Dean, who, after the *Wigeon* struggled into Port Jackson, obtained a passage in the American barque *Sacramento*, loaded with Newcastle coal.

'Then, turning to the right, round Clark's Point, we beheld . . . the masts and yards of hundreds of vessels from all parts of the world looking like a forest of dry trees, the extent of which may be gathered from the fact that in September, 1850, there were seven hundred vessels in the harbour and one hundred more arrived within five weeks.'[29]

But for those who arrived during the rainy season the weather was a more lasting memory. 'Dear Elspeth,' wrote John Jamison, a Sussex Street butcher, to his wife back in Sydney, 'I am very sorry to inform you that I arrived in a very bad time of the year, when mountains are all covered with snow and rain falling in torrents; and what is worse than all, nothing to cover our heads but a cold canvas tent, with ground for the floor; therefore you that are in a comfortable house need not envy our comforts in the gold regions of California.'[30]

'. . . I landed once more on terra firma, and soon found myself knee deep in mud,' Thomas Hinigan wrote. '. . . During the first week I was daily on shore in search of a situation, but was unsuccessful. I soon obtained, however, a severe cold, which was followed by dysentery. . . . It rained from the 18th January to the 27th, two fine days then intervened, and it rained again until the 6th February. The remainder of the month was very fine, and every one thought the rainy season was over. Not so, however, for on the 1st March it set in again as bad as ever and continued until yesterday [7th March]. I have not up to the present time earned a cent. . . .'[31]

New arrivals were shocked by the dearness of food and other articles. Hinigan claimed that 'for what a man could get in Sydney for one pound per week, he will have to pay ten pounds here,'[32] and Jamison, writing three months earlier than Hinigan, said beef, 'of such a quality I would scarcely give it to my dog', cost one shilling per pound, bread one shilling and sixpence a loaf of one and a half pounds, tea four shillings a pound and sugar a shilling a pound. Spirits were plentiful and cheap, but vegetables he had never seen. The rent of a house of one room cost the equivalent of twenty pounds sterling a month, and board and lodgings ran from sixteen to thirty dollars per week.[33]

'After a residence here of seven months,' wrote another Australian from San Francisco on 10th November 1849, 'I am led, from my own observation, to believe that if any one hundred Australians who may leave the colonies in health were correctly accounted for at the end of a year, it would be found that about twenty have died, thirty have been so injured in their constitution that their recovery is hopeless, twenty will have disappeared altogether and cannot be accounted for, ten will be about as well off as when they left Sydney and ten may have money – and, if anything, I think this rather too favourable a view of the case.'[34]

At first work was plentiful and wages high, but as thousands upon thousands of immigrants arrived, there came unemployment and lower wages. Mining was a lottery. 'A man may in one month realize a fortune,' wrote Hinigan,[35] 'may work three months without making more than his expenses. It requires at least one hundred and fifty dollars to carry a man to the mines.'

The consequence was that many were so disgusted on arrival that they at once set about getting home again. 'I am here now,' wrote a coachman from San Francisco on 25th February 1850, just after his arrival from Sydney, 'but wishes myself back again. When you arrive at this port you have five shillings a head to pay before you land – then the captain and supercargo charges you so much per ton for landing your luggage. When you get ashore there is neither house nor place to go to. Friends do not know you. At present you would see thousands walking along the beach starving . . . many more returning by the first convenience. . . . My wife and I are engaged to proceed up the Sacramento to the diggings at very trifling wages. As soon as I can make up enough to return, I will.'[36]

William Shaw was in California less than three months and was then glad to work his passage back in the *Mazeppa*, leaving San Francisco on New Year's Day, 1850. As a sidelight on the inflationary prices, it is interesting to note that the *Mazeppa's* captain found it cheaper to ballast his ship with sand and rum than with the more usual stone ballast.[37]

The barque *Ajax*, which reached Sydney on 24th March 1850, was worked back by one-time gold-seekers anxious to return to the land whence they had set out, and sixteen of her nineteen steerage passengers were people who had set out from Australia earlier in high hopes of making their fortunes.[38] More and more emigrants returned as the year drew on.

But, of course, there were many Australians and New Zealanders whose financial circumstances prevented their return or who had faith in California's future and stuck it out until they made good. Thomas Hinigan, despite illness and unemployment, remained and seems in the end to have been successful, since he was joined by his wife and children.

A couple who journeyed to California from Victoria for their honeymoon come also into this category. An old diary kept by the father of Mary Hobler, the bride, tells their story.[39] Under the date of 1st June 1850, we find recorded: 'I today wrote to Mr. Finis [?] in Sydney to have a marquee made and forwarded against Mr. Strack is ready to start and I suppose there can nothing better be done in the premises, as the lawyers call it, than that Mary should be married and seek her fortune with him in the El Dorado. I must confess I would rather he went alone if he was not too completely Irish to be trusted among wild young fellows, with his pockets full of gold and no one he cared for at his side to put some restraint upon his natural habit of carelessness and gaiety. It is, no doubt, a finer field for his exertions than has ever before been open to him, and as he has for many years been waiting for a chance to do well in the world and to take upon himself the cares of a merino man, I do not feel disposed to withstand them, and, after all, it is less of a venture than my coming to Van Diemen's Land from England, having all but mere farming matters to learn, a wife and two children.

'They have experience of bush life, an ample supply of provisions and anything they can want for a long time; will take a covered cart to travel to the gold diggings in and a comfortable lined marquee to be sent there to house them, and they are sure to have immediate neighbours that they know, who on the same errand leave this country and will be glad to live near together for mutual protection. I would like well to join the party if all else was convenient and certainly will if they do well and the price of wool does not keep up.'[40]

On 13th June Clark, a carrier, called at the Hobler homestead to take Mary's piano to Melbourne, where it was to be sold. But it seemed the couple would never get away. They were to have sailed from Melbourne in the *Spartan*, but her captain accepted a charter to sail from Launceston instead. Strack went to Melbourne, but returned on 28th June 'bringing a sad account of the unruly conduct of a hundred and twenty passengers in the *William Watson*; the captain seemed afraid of his customers and was anxious to dispossess them of their firearms before he put to sea'.[41]

By 8th July Mary Hobler's father was growing uneasy about the couple obtaining a vessel for California from Melbourne. 'It is such a humbug of a place,' he wrote. 'It will add much to the expense of the voyage if they are obliged to go elsewhere for one.'[42] This is what they had to do, however. Mary and her carefree Irish suitor were married on 10th July, but not until 27th August did they board the steamer *Shamrock* for Sydney, on the first leg of their honeymoon voyage to California.

'Poor Mary held up well to the last moment,' wrote her father.[43] 'I hope she will never have cause of grief from her enterprise other than that which was so natural at leaving all her friends to accompany her husband to a strange land and people. I gave him a hundred and fifty pounds in cash to cover her expenses and twelve dozen champagne, which sell at sixty shillings a dozen there readily, and my new London revolving rifle, given to me by Mr. Backer, which will raise him a good sum there. It cost thirty-five guineas in London. He has a tent or marquee, rattin lined and divided, a capital tilted spring cart and harness for two horses – everything he can require for a year to come, so that I hope the results of their venture will be satisfactory. With prudence on his part, they can't fail to do well.'

The newlyweds, as Mary's first letter disclosed, had a 'very seasick voyage' to Sydney in the *Shamrock*, an iron paddlewheeler of 201 tons.[44] They crossed the Pacific in the *Inchinnan*, having a quiet voyage and speaking well of their treatment.[45] The Stracks, if they ever went to the goldfields, did not remain there long, and by May 1850 they had settled on a small holding of twenty acres three miles from San Francisco, and had converted it into a profitable market garden. The reckless Irishman was not quite as wild as his father-in-law had imagined!

Hobler followed the honeymooners to San Francisco,

but he did not leave Melbourne until March 1851, by which time the Californian gold mania had subsided.[46]

Yet even at this late date there were still some people anxious to emigrate to California. There were, for instance, more than seventy passengers aboard the British ship *Mary Catherine*, of 365 tons, when she sailed from Sydney on 8th April 1851. Her commander was Henry Thomas Fox, portion of whose private log of the voyage has survived in private ownership, perhaps the most complete record extant of a voyage from Australia to San Francisco around the time of the gold rush.[47]

The *Mary Catherine* got under way in Sydney Cove at daylight on 8th April, but with light airs and a short sea from the eastward she spent two hours between the Heads while the police mustered and checked her passengers. At noon Fox discharged the pilot near North Head and the *Mary Catherine* headed out slowly into the Tasman. There was little wind and 'tolerably smooth water', but few passengers were on deck to watch the land gradually disappear from view. Most, like the captain's wife and child, were seasick, and those who were not were down below, celebrating their departure and drinking to their future. Fox records that they 'were rather inclined to be troublesome about the arrangement of their berths, but the officers managed to quiet them without my going below, much to my satisfaction'.

The wind was light and fickle and, being mostly easterly, the *Mary Catherine's* progress was at first slow. She gained but thirty-eight miles in the twenty-four hours to noon on 10th April, and then lost six miles during the following twenty-four hours. By noon on 14th April, the sixth day out, she had covered only some two hundred and twenty-five miles and was in latitude 39° 44' S. and longitude 158° 33' E. Probably her passengers did not mind the slow progress; for the unusually settled and fine weather meant smooth seas and comparatively little movement in the ship. Even the captain's wife, Isobel Fox, who was a very poor sailor, was able to walk the poop in the evening. The passengers, having formed a band of two fiddles, a fife and a triangle, enjoyed dances. On the evening of the 15th, when the light wind became westerly, enabling the studding sails to be set for the first time since leaving Sydney, the steerage passengers held several dances, while the few cabin passengers 'danced a quadrille on the poop, such as it was, the doctor's lady and I and Isobel and Mr. Lowe, the second mate, forming the set'. Isobel Fox also danced a schottische and a polka with her husband, 'which', Fox tells us, 'is what even in my most sanguine moments I never expected she would accomplish in so short a time'.

Next day the weather changed, and with strong, squally southerlies the *Mary Catherine* began to make faster progress. However, not until 10 a.m. on 26th April, eighteen days out from Sydney, was the coast of the North Island of New Zealand sighted in the vicinity of North Cape. The pilot was picked up at 5 p.m. on 2nd May and, after having spent the night at anchor inside North Head, the *Mary Catherine* beat up Auckland Harbour next morning to anchor abreast the watering-place below Fort Britomart at eight o'clock. She had made a slow passage of twenty-five days from Sydney.

The *Mary Catherine* resumed her voyage on the 13th, getting under way at 10 a.m. As she proceeded down harbour with a light southerly wind, a search of the 'tween-decks and coal hole brought three stowaways to light. They were sent back to shore when the pilot was dropped off Rangitoto Island at 2 p.m. The *Mary Catherine* then kept away for the Cape Colville passage under all studding sails. The weather was rougher and the winds stronger than on the run from Sydney and the ship made good progress. But she was no flier. Indeed, she reminded Captain Fox of the description of a vessel of the same name he had read in Dana's *Two Years before the Mast* – a barque with a high poop and top-gallant forecastle, and sawed-off square stem and stern, like a true English tea-wagon and with a run like a sugar box. 'She had studding sails out alow and aloft, with a light but steady breeze,' recorded Dana, 'and her captain said he could not get more than four knots out of her and thought he should have a long passage. We were going six, on an easy bowline.' Fox thought this description fitted his own vessel so exactly that he wondered whether the *Mary Catherine* seen by Dana could be the ship he now commanded, but the latter had not been built until 1836, the year in which the other *Mary Catherine* had been seen by Dana, who had described her as 'an old, damaged-looking craft'.

By 26th May – Fox had not altered the dates in his private log after crossing the meridian of 180° from Greenwich and coming into west longitude on the afternoon of 15th May – the *Mary Catherine* was far enough to the eastward to fetch Tahiti and accordingly Fox altered course to the N.N.E. to pass near that island. At noon the *Mary Catherine's* position was lat. obs. 30° 39′ S., long. chr. 155- 00′ W. The wind had moderated and for the first time since leaving New Zealand the musicians and singers resumed their concerts that evening. The next evening the dancers also were on the poop again.

To pass the time, some of the women passengers had turned their hands to producing a shipboard newspaper, and on 31st May, which happened to be the captain's thirty-second birthday, the first number of the *Flying Fish*, 'a little journal of fun and merriment', as Fox described it, made its appearance. The captain gave the passengers some wine and other liquor with which to drink to his birthday, but a number of them, not content with the one toast, got drunk and the evening ended with a few fights.

In dark and lowering weather Tahiti was sighted at daylight on 1st June, the nineteenth day out from Auckland. The island was higher than Fox had expected, and when the *Mary Catherine* rounded the West Point at noon a mile off the reef, and opened out the town and harbour of Papeete, she was unexpectedly becalmed. Fortunately, a breeze from the E.N.E. sprang up at 3 p.m. and the *Mary Catherine* stood to the northward in thick, misty weather. By the following afternoon the ship was running dead before a gale, carrying no more canvas than close-reefed topsails and foresail.

'The weather was so much worse than anything I could have expected in this region at this season,' wrote Fox that day, 'that I almost feared at one time we should have a hurricane and but that I knew it was not the season for them, I should have made preparations. As it was, I sent down the royal yards and mizen top-gallant sail having been blown to pieces in taking it in, I sent down its yard also.' The gale, however, quickly blew itself out : the wind lulled rapidly after dusk and by midnight it was calm, with a clear sky.

As the *Mary Catherine* ran through the tropics, meeting occasional squalls and much rain, there were the normal shipboard troubles of the sailing era. Tempers frayed quickly in the enervating heat. The doctor quarrelled with a passenger whose wife he was treating, and for several days Fox feared that a woman passenger who had drunk chloride of zinc in mistake for water would die. At 2 a.m. on 13th June the captain found his chief officer, Mr. Fittock, asleep on the poop during his watch, and six days later detected him again in the same offence. On 25th June – a day earlier according to local time – the *Mary Catherine* anchored at Honolulu, forty-three days out from Auckland, 'a better passage than any vessel for some time'.

On the evening of 2nd July the *Mary Catherine* hauled off from the wharf. Next morning a search disclosed the presence of two stowaways. They were sent ashore and at noon the ship got under way. Two hours after she had run through the reef and dropped the pilot four more stowaways came on deck from their hiding-places, and as they were all sailors, they were put immediately to work. The *Mary Catherine* was now a very full ship. Her owner, Mr. Nathan, who had travelled in her from

Sydney, had remained at Honolulu with another passenger, but five additional cabin and a number of steerage passengers had been squeezed aboard.

Captain Fox's private log ends on 24th July, when the *Mary Catherine* was twenty-one days out from Honolulu. Those twenty-one days had been mostly uneventful. In the early hours of the morning of 12th July, however, the captain had again found the troublesome Mr. Fittock asleep on watch. At the time a strange barque, which turned out to be a Dutchman, the *Sphynx*, seventy-nine days out from Batavia to San Francisco, was in sight. Fox and a passenger lunched aboard the Dutch barque, and that evening the latter's master, Captain Wigman, and his sole passenger, a Scotchman named Campbell, dined aboard the *Mary Catherine*.

Flies, 'which bite or sting most atrociously', troubled the passengers for two or three days, and at 6 p.m. on 20th July the *Mary Catherine* passed through the largest school of Portuguese men-of-war Fox had ever seen in one place, although, since the ship was in latitude 40°, he would not have expected to have encountered them at all. But for eleven days the sea had been so tranquil that 'the most fragile of all barks, a New Hollander's bark canoe, without the slightest exaggeration, might have come all the way'. The only untoward incident was a quarrel between two women in the steerage which ended up in a general mêlée.

The *Mary Catherine* arrived off San Francisco in company with the Boston ship *Tagus*, which was 179 days out from New York. There was a thick fog when the two vessels took on their pilots. The *Mary Catherine*, which was in the lead, anchored for safety, but the *Tagus*, which had been a quarter of a mile astern, kept on for the harbour entrance. So thick was the fog that those in the *Mary Catherine* could not see the American ship as she passed or as she ran ashore a mile away. They did not sight her until next morning, when the fog had cleared and the *Mary Catherine* entered port. It was on

Where many Australians and New Zealanders collected their mail — the post-office at San Francisco
(Lithograph by William Endicott & Co., after a drawing by H. F. Cox. New York Public Library)

Two sections from a panoramic photograph of the
signs of human life in this panorama is one of its
Francisco, by courtesy o

…id up in San Francisco harbour. The absence of all
…able features (Society of Californian Pioneers, San
…ncisco Maritime Museum)

Sacramento City in 1849. The paddlewheel steamer is the *Senator* (Lithograph by William Endicott & Co., after a drawing by G. V. Cooper. New York Public Library)

3rd August that she anchored in San Francisco harbour, and she was then 116 days out from Sydney.[48]

Fox and the *Mary Catherine* returned to Sydney. Except for three men, her crew had deserted her immediately on her arrival, but Fox managed to get together another crew, and on the afternoon of 29th August the *Mary Catherine*, with a small number of passengers, beat out of San Francisco against a breeze from the south-west. She reached Honolulu on 24th September and arrived back at Port Jackson on 9th November.[49]

PROBABLY BETWEEN seven and eight thousand people sailed from Australia and New Zealand for San Francisco while the Californian gold rush was on. The incomplete figures of passengers listed in the appendixes give a total of over six thousand two hundred from Australia and of almost four hundred and ninety from New Zealand, but, as already mentioned,[1] the latter figure omits, apparently, many steerage passengers.

By the beginning of 1851, however, the tide was flowing in the opposite direction. Large numbers of disillusioned gold-seekers were arriving in Australia, many of them men who had sailed for San Francisco from Australia only a few months earlier in gay spirits and with high hopes. That most of those who now reached Australia from California had failed to make their fortunes is proved by the preponderance of steerage passengers. In January, for instance, five vessels from San Francisco arrived at Port Jackson with twenty-two cabin and at least one hundred and seventy-five steerage passengers.[2]

Among the passengers who returned to Sydney in the brig *Emma* on 7th January was Edward Hammond Hargraves, who had sailed for California in July 1849. A small squatter on the Bathurst plains, he had fallen on hard times during the recession of the 1840s and had emigrated to San Francisco in the hope of repairing his fortunes on the goldfields. In this he failed, and on

23rd November 1850, he left San Francisco in the *Emma*, a barque of 199 tons that carried seven cabin and about sixty steerage passengers.[3]

On 5th February Hargraves set out from Sydney on horseback to return to the Bathurst district. Five days' riding brought him to Guyong, where he engaged the services of an eighteen-years-old youth named Lister as an assistant and guide. During the next few weeks Hargraves, using techniques he had learned in California, discovered gold, notably at Ophir. His discovery, like that of Marshall, is shrouded now in legend, and the exact circumstances are largely a matter of surmise.[4]

Not until 15th May 1851 was Hargraves's discovery publicly announced in the *Sydney Morning Herald*, and immediately hundreds of people began the trek to Ophir on foot, on horseback and in carts or coaches. New South Wales now witnessed what California had seen in the first weeks after Marshall's find on the Sacramento.

Publication of the news that Hargraves had washed the first pan of gold-bearing gravel in the Bathurst district on 12th February stimulated the quest for gold in the Port Phillip district. James Esmond, who, like Hargraves, had returned from California early in the year, found gold in Victoria on 1st July.

Australia now became the new El Dorado of the world. California was forgotten – Marshall's discovery belonged already to the past. The tide of emigration from Australia became a flood of immigration. Once the news had travelled overseas, crowded vessels began to race for Australia. From England, Ireland, Scotland, China, Germany, America and many other countries thousands of would-be miners began in 1852 to reach the mainland ports of Australia. Very soon the masts of deserted sailing vessels in Port Phillip Bay presented a leafless forest as extensive as once had greeted newcomers by sea to San Francisco. In the decade between 1851 and 1861 Australia's population rose from 400,000 to almost 1,200,000.[5]

But the story of the great influx of miners to Australia and of the vessels which brought them does not belong to this book. It is a story entirely separate from that of Australia's gold fleet to California. But it reveals the irony of thousands of Australians flocking to California in 1849 and 1850 when vast quantities of gold lay in the gullies and creeks of Australia waiting only the miner's pick and pan.

REFERENCES

CHAPTER 1

1. Quoted in *California: A Guide to the Golden State* (compiled and written by Federal Writers' Project of the Works Progress Administration for the State of California, New York: 1947), 54.
2. Arthur H. Clark, *The Clipper Ship Era* (New York: 1911), 100–1.
3. Georgia Willis Read (ed.), *A Pioneer of 1850 : George Willis Read, 1819–1880* (Boston: 1927), viii, citing Hittell, *Hist. California* (San Francisco: 1898), iii, 44, and Soule, Gibbon and Nisbet, *Annals of San Francisco* (New York: 1855), 300.
4. Ibid., citing E. G. Squier, *Notes on Central America* (New York: 1855), 300.
5. Ibid.
6. Ibid.
7. Clark, op. cit., 103.
8. Robert Glass Cleland, *The Cattle on a Thousand Hills* (New York: 1941), p. 3.
9. John Walton Caughey, *California* (New York: 1953), passim; Robert Glass Cleland, *From Wilderness to Empire: A History of California* (edited by Glenn S. Dumke; New York: 1959), passim. The population figures come from Federal or State censuses, but in the circumstances of the times the strict accuracy of those for 1850 and 1852 are questionable. As approximations, however, they may be accepted.

CHAPTER 2

1. Harbourmaster's Records, Honolulu (hereafter abbreviated to H.R., Hon.), 5 Sep. 1848; *Sandwich Island News*, 7 Sep. 1848; *Polynesian*, 23 Sep. 1848, 75 (advt.), 30 Sep. 1848, 79.

2. H.R., Hon., 7 Nov. 1848; *Polynesian*, 11 Nov. 1848.

3. Shipping Reports, Arrivals, Mitchell Library (hereafter abbreviated to S.R., Arr., Mit. Lib.), sub *Phantom*, 21 Dec. 1848; *Sydney Morning Herald* (hereafter abbreviated to *S.M.H.*), 20 Dec., 1848.

4. S.R., Arr., Mit. Lib., sub *Despatch*, 22 Dec. 1848; *S.M.H.*, 23 Dec. 1848.

5. Customs House, Sydney, Ship Registers (hereafter abbreviated to C.H., Syd., S.R.), 7/47; S.R., Arr., Mit. Lib., sub *Phantom*, 21 Dec. 1848; *S.M.H.*, 21 Dec. 1848.

6. C.H., Syd., S.R., 14/48; S.R., Arr., Mit. Lib., sub *Despatch*, 22 Dec. 1848; *S.M.H.*, 23 Dec. 1848.

7. *S.M.H.*, 21 Dec. 1848.

8. *Melbourne Daily News* (hereafter abbreviated to *M.D.N.*), 30 Dec. 1848.

CHAPTER 3

1. *S.M.H.*, 4 Jan. 1849.

2. Towns to Brooks, 17 Jan. 1849, Towns MS., Mit. Lib., Uncatalogued set 307, item 68.

3. *The Life and Adventures of Captain William Collin* (Brisbane : 1914), 105.

4. *S.M.H.*, 8 Jan. 1849.

5. Towns to D. C. Mackey & Co., 29 Nov. 1848; Towns to Russell & Sturgis, 30 Nov. 1848; Towns to Frederick Strachan, 22 Dec. 1848, Towns MS., Mit. Lib., Uncatalogued set 307, item 58.

6. Towns to Goldsmith, 23 Dec. 1848, Towns M.S., ibid.

7. Commercial Intelligence, *S.M.H.*, 23 Dec. 1848 and 13 Jan. 1849.

8. Towns to A. Browne & Co., Melbourne, 9 and 22 Feb. 1849, Towns MS., Mit. Lib., Uncatalogued set 307, item 58.

9. Towns to J. Smith, East Maitland, 10 Jan. 1849, ibid.

10. Towns to R. Harrison, Singleton, 11 Jan. 1849, ibid.

11. Towns to J. Smith, East Maitland, 10 Jan. 1849, ibid.

12. Towns to Editor, *Mercury*, Maitland, 11 Jan. 1849, ibid.

13. *Britannia and Trades Advocate*, 18 Jan. 1849.

14. *M.D.N.*, passim.

15. *Argus*, 2 Feb. 1849.

16. *South Australian Register*, passim.

CHAPTER 4

1. Towns to Brooks, 17 Jan. 1849, Towns MS., Mit. Lib., Uncatalogued set 307, item 68.
2. Towns to Dr. Silver, 20 Jan. 1849, ibid., item 58.
3. C.H., Syd., S.R. 23/47; Tas. Archives, Hobart, Acc. No. 1/30.
4. *S.M.H.*, 6 Aug. 1849; letter to author, 12 Sep. 1957, from Agnes C. Conrad, Archivist, Bd. of Cmmrs. of Public Arch., Honolulu; H.R., Hon., 10 Apr. 1849; *Polynesian*, 14 Apr. 1849.
5. C.H., Syd., S.R., 16/42, 54/44, 27/45.
6. *S.M.H.*, 20 Aug. 1849.
7. *S.M.H.*, 6 Aug. 1849.
8. *S.M.H.*, 3 Oct. 1849, 29 Apr. 1850.
9. Towns to Lodge, 10 Aug. 1849, Towns MS., Mit. Lib., Uncatalogued set 307, item 59.
10. Lodge to Towns, 5 Oct. 1849, ibid., item 89.
11. *S.M.H.*, 6 Aug. 1849.
12. *S.M.H.*, 12 Mar. 1849.
13. *S.M.H.*, 13 Mar. 1849.
14. *S.M.H.*, 24 Mar. 1849.
15. *S.M.H.*, 6 and 7 May 1849.
16. *S.M.H.*, 22 May 1849.
17. *S.M.H.*, 11 and 30 June and 13 July 1849.
18. *S.M.H.*, 11, 21 and 25 May 1849.
19. *S.M.H.*, 12, 24 and 28 May 1849.
20. Appendixes 1, 2, 3, 4.
21. *S.M.H.*, 6 and 29 June 1849; C.H., Syd., S.R., 14/43, 77/48.

CHAPTER 5

1. Grahame Farr, *West Country Passenger Steamers* (London: 1956), 27, 52, 62–3, 279, 296; C.H., Syd., S.R., 3/47, 33/47, 68/48.
2. S.R., Arr., Mit. Lib., s.a. 1842; *S.M.H.*, 26 Mar. 1842.
3. *S.M.H.*, 26 Mar. 1842.
4. C.H., Syd., S.R., 3/47, 33/47.
5. *S.M.H.*, 27 Sep. 1847.
6. *South Australian Register*, 6 Nov. 1847.
7. *S.M.H.*, 23 Nov. 1847.
8. Jour. R.A.H.S., xxi, 330-1; Tas. Arch., CSO 24/101/3162; *S.M.H.*, 20 July 1849.
9. *S.M.H.*, 20 July 1848.
10. Towns to Robert Brooks, 24 July 1849, Towns MS., Mit. Lib., Uncatalogued set 307, item 69.

11. Do. to do., 28 July 1849, Towns MS., ibid.

12. John H. Morrison, *History of American Steam Navigation* (New York: 1958), 396–7; Erik Heyl, *Early American Steamers* (Buffalo: 1953), 387–8; Richard C. McKay, *South Street: A Maritime History of New York* (New York: 1934), 281–4.

13. C.H., Syd., S.R., 68/48.

14. *S.M.H.*, 8 Nov. 1853.

15. *S.M.H.*, 3 and 6 Sep. 1849.

CHAPTER 6

1. *Britannia and Trades Advocate*, 22 Feb. 1849. Possibly the W. L. Goodwin was William Lushington Goodwin, who at one time was master of the convict ship *Kains*. See Charles Bateson, *The Convict Ships* (Glasgow: 1959), 221–6.

2. Ibid., 22 Feb. 1849.

3. Tas. Arch., CSO 24/95/ Acc. No. 2/282.

4. Ibid.

5. Tas. Arch., CSO 24/95/2906, Michael Innes to Col. Sec., 22 Feb. 1849; memo. from Chief Constable, same date.

6. Ibid.

7. Tas. Arch., Acc. No. 2/282.

8. L. Norman, *Pioneer Shipping of Tasmania* (Hobart: n.d., but c 1938), 25. I have not been able to trace the present whereabouts of Miss Chapman's letters.

9. E.g., L. S. Bethell, *The Story of Port Dalrymple* (Hobart: n.d.), 54.

10. Col. Sec. Pap., Mit. Lib. MSS. The letters of the Water Police Magistrate, Principal Superintendent of Convicts, etc., are gathered together in the file for Magistrates and Gaolers, 1849. They comprise: 4/6463, 6724, 7022, 728, 7286.

11. Tas. Arch., Acc. No. 2/276.

12. A detailed description of the *Helen*, issued after her seizure, will be found in Col. Sec. Pap., Mit. Lib., 50/2199, which was published in the *Government Gazette*, 13 Mar. 1850, and *S.M.H.*, 14 Mar. 1850.

13. W. T. Pritchard, *Polynesian Reminiscences* (London: 1866), 187 sq.

14. Ibid., 194–5.

15. Col. Sec. Pap., Mit. Lib., 50/4726, Water Police to Col. Sec., 11 May 1850.

16. Ibid., 50/4964, Water Police Report, 20 May 1850.

17. Full details of the *Helen's* seizure, including affidavits by Captain Griffiths, West, Crepo and others, describing events, will be found in Col. Sec. Pap., Mit. Lib., 50/2199, 50/7523.
18. Col. Sec. Pap., Mit. Lib., Water Police Magistrate to Col. Sec., 23 Feb. 1851 (51/1876), 22 Apr. 1851 (51/4026).
19. Ibid., 52/10509, 10638; *S.M.H.*, Feb. 1853.
20. *New Zealander*, 6 Feb. 1850; *S.M.H.*, 13 Apr. 1850. This *William and James*, presumably, was a smaller ship than the vessel of the same name which sailed from Auckland, N.Z., for San Francisco on 14 Mar. 1850 with seven passengers.

CHAPTER 7

1. Towns to Goldsmith, 23 Dec. 1848, Towns MS., Mit. Lib., Uncatalogued set 307, item 58.
2. C.H., Syd., S.R., 2/42, 28/45 (*British Sovereign*), 15/42, 10/45 (*Lucy Ann*), 82/43 (*Terror*), 83/43 (*Edward*), 11/44 (*Fame*), 15/44 (*Juno*), 33/44 (*William*), 36/44 (*Margaret*), 37/44 (*Velocity*), 77/45 (*Rebecca*), 37/42, 82/45 (*Portenia*), 3/47, 33/47 (*Juno*, steamer). I have not located the registers of the *Seahorse* and the *Cornubia*.
3. *S.M.H.*, 11 Feb. 1850.
4. John Webster, *The Last Cruise of the Wanderer, R.Y.S.* (Sydney: c. 1866).
5. Letter to Editor from L. W. S. Wright, *S.M.H.*, 11 Jan. 1960.
6. *S.M.H.*, passim.
7. C.H., Syd., S.R., 57/46. The Portland Bay registers are missing.
8. Ibid., 74/47.
9. Ibid., 56/49.
10. Ibid., 56/48.
11. Ibid., 77/49.
12. Supreme Court Pap., Bankruptcies, Reg. 2, No. 1958, Mit. Lib., passim.
13. *S.M.H.*, 6 Oct. 1849.
14. Supreme Court Pap., Bankruptcies, Reg. 2, No. 1958, Mit. Lib., passim, but particularly examinations of George Atkinson and George Merrett.
15. Ibid., passim.
16. Ibid., passim; *S.M.H.*, 27 and 29 Oct. 1849.
17. Ibid., passim; *S.M.H.*, 5, 6 and 19 Nov. 1849.
18. Ibid., passim.
19. Ibid., examination of George Atkinson, 2 Aug. 1850.
20. C.H., Syd., S.R., 33/41.

21. Supreme Court Pap., Bankruptcies, No. 1132, Mit. Lib.
22. *S.M.H.*, 31 Oct. 1849.

CHAPTER 8

1. *M.D.N.*, 17 Jan. 1849.
2. *Argus*, 19 Jan. 1849; *Melbourne Morning Herald*, 20 Jan. 1849; *Port Phillip Gazette*, 20 Jan. 1849; *M.D.N.*, 20 Jan. 1849.
3. *Melbourne Morning Herald*, 20 Jan. 1849.
4. *M.D.N.*, 20 Jan. 1849.
5. *Argus*, 23 Jan. 1849.
6. *Port Phillip Gazette*, 24 and 31 Jan. 1849; *Melbourne Morning Herald*, 25 Jan. 1849.
7. *S.M.H.*, 20 June 1849.
8. *S.M.H.*, 21 June 1849.
9. *S.M.H.*, 22 June 1849.
10. *S.M.H.*, 30 June 1849.
11. C.H., Syd., S.R., 1/40; *S.M.H.*, 5 July 1849.
12. *S.M.H.*, 5 July 1849.
13. *S.M.H.*, 11 Aug. 1849.
14. *S.M.H.*, 15 Sep. 1849.
15. C.H., Syd., S.R., 93/49, 105/49; *S.M.H.*, 20 Sep. 1849.
16. *S.M.H.*, 20 Sep. 1849.
17. *S.M.H.*, 25 Oct. 1849.
18. *S.M.H.*, 26 Oct. 1849.
19. *S.M.H.*, 20 Nov. 1849.
20. C.H., Syd., S.R., 93/49; 105/49.
21. *S.M.H.*, 13 and 18 Dec. 1849.

CHAPTER 9

1. *S.M.H.*, 30 June 1849.
2. Towns to T. Collins, 27 June 1849, Towns MS., Mit. Lib., Uncatalogued set 307, item 59.
3. Towns to Major D'Arcy Wentworth, 28 June 1849; to John Pike, 28 June 1849; to W. C. Wentworth, 29 June 1849, ibid.
4. Towns to Lodge, 26 Oct. 1849, ibid.
5. Towns to T. Collins, 27 June 1849, ibid.
6. Towns to E. ?Charnell, 23 Aug. 1849, and to Russell & Sturgis, Manila, 5 Sep. 1849, ibid.
7. Pearse to Brooks, 31 Aug. 1849, ibid., item 89.

8. Towns to Major Wentworth, 28 June 1849, ibid., item 59.
9. Towns to Blyth, 27 July 1849, and to Icely, 6 Aug. 1849, ibid.
10. Towns to Capt. Chaurell, 10 Aug. 1849, and to Edwin Hickey, 23 Aug. 1849, ibid.
11. *S.M.H.*, 7 Aug. 1849.
12. Towns to Robert Brooks, 28 July and 8 Aug. 1849, Towns MS., Mit. Lib., Uncatalogued set 307, item 69.
13. Agreement, 16 Aug. 1849, between Towns and Aldrich, ibid., item 89.
14. Memo. of Agreement between Towns and Collard, n.d., but probably 28 or 29 Aug. 1849, ibid., item 59.
15. *S.M.H.*, 20 Aug. 1849.
16. *S.M.H.*, 28 Aug. 1849.
17. *S.M.H.*, 21 Sep. 1849.
18. Pearse to Brooks, 31 Aug. 1849, Towns MS., Mit. Lib., Uncatalogued set 307, item 89.
19. Towns to Edward Parker, 22 Aug. 1849, and to Laurence Potts, 22 Aug. 1849, ibid., item 59.
20. *S.M.H.*, 15 Nov. 1849.
21. *S.M.H.*, 24, 26 and 29 Dec. 1849.
22. *S.M.H.*, 25 and 26 Jan. 1849, 2, 7 and 8 Feb. 1849.
23. *S.M.H.*, 14 and 29 Jan. 1849.
24. *S.M.H.*, 2 Aug. 1849.
25. *S.M.H.*, 20 Aug. and 6 Sep. 1849.
26. *S.M.H.*, 4 July 1849.
27. *S.M.H.*, 18 Aug., 17 Sep., 25 Aug., and 15 Sep. 1849.
28. Towns to Brooks, 12 Sep. 1849, Towns MS., Mit. Lib., Uncatalogued set 307, item 69.
29. *S.M.H.*, 5 Sep. 1849.
30. H.R., Hon., 1849.
31. Tas. Arch., Acc. No. 8/1462.
32. Vernon Smith, *Sailing Ship Captains* (Pioneers' Assn. of S.A.), 8–10.
33. *South Australian Register*, 18 and 25 Apr. 1849.
34. Ibid., 6 June 1849.
35. Ibid., 8 Dec. 1849.
36. City Librarian, Auckland Public Libraries, to author, 5 Apr. 1957, with list of ships departing for California, and subsequent interchange of correspondence.

CHAPTER 10

1. C.H., Syd., S.R., 5/48.

2. Ibid., 5/48 (*Phantom*), 61/40, 47/43, 44/46 (*Georgiana*).
3. Ibid., 70/49, 74/49.
4. Ibid., 5/48.
5. Ibid., 61/40, 47/43, 44/46, 70/49, 74/49.
6. N.Z. Ship Registers, Auckland, 9/49.
7. *S.M.H.*, 11 June 1850.
8. C.H., Syd., S.R., 5/48.
9. *San Francisco Herald*, 2 July 1850.
10. Ante, p. 106.
11. *San Francisco California Courier*, 2 July 1850.
12. City Librarian, Auckland Public Libraries, to author, 5 Apr. 1957, with list of ships departing for California; San Francisco arrival date furnished by Bancroft Library, University of California, and Society of California Pioneers, San Francisco.
13. Ibid.
14. C.H., Syd., S.R., 71/49 (*Giraffe*), 68/49 (*Fame*), 35/49(*Margaret*), 100/49 (*Lord Hobart*), 37/49 (*Bee*).
15. *S.M.H.*, 31 Aug. 1850.
16. C.H., Syd., S.R., 55/45, 17/47.
17. Ante, p. 67.
18. *S.M.H.*, 12 Apr. 1850; Chas. W. N. Ingram and P. Owen Wheatley, *Shipwrecks: New Zealand Disasters, 1795–1950* (Wellington, N.Z.: 1951), 56.
19. *S.M.H.*, 29 Apr. 1850; *Honolulu Times*, 27 Mar. 1850, quoted in *S.M.H.*, 10 May 1850; *Polynesian*, 30 Mar. 1850, quoted ibid., 21 May 1850.
20. *New Zealander*, 2 Mar. 1850; City Librarian, Auckland Public Libraries, to the author, 1 Aug. 1857.
21. Information supplied by the Society of California Pioneers, San Francisco.
22. City Librarian, Auckland Public Libraries, to the author, 5 Apr. 1957, with list of ships departing for California; H.R., Hon.; Harry O'May, *Wooden Hookers of Hobart Town* (Hobart: n.d., but c. 1957), 62; W. Lawson, *Blue Gum Clippers and Whale Ships of Tasmania* (Melbourne: 1949), 93, 241.
23. City Librarian, Auckland Public Libraries, to author, 5 Apr. 1957, with list of ships departing for California; O'May, op. cit., 62; Lawson, op. cit., 117, 165.
24. Unfortunately, I have mislaid my reference to this report, but I fancy it appeared in a New Zealand paper.
25. Information supplied by the Society of California Pioneers, San Francisco.
26. *S.M.H.*, 18 Sep. 1850, quoting *San Francisco Herald*, 24 June 1850.
27. *S.M.H.*, 9 Nov. 1850.

28. C.H., Syd., S.R., 82/47.
29. *S.M.H.*, 16 Dec. 1850 (account by J. H. Green, a passenger), 17 Dec. 1850 (statement by Capt. Patrick).

CHAPTER 11

1. *S.M.H.*, 20 May 1850.
2. Robert Glass Cleland, *From Wilderness to Empire* (New York: 1944), 264; Gertrude Atherton, *Golden Gate Country* (New York: 1945), 90.
3. Josiah Royce, *California from the Conquest in 1846 to the Second Vigilance Committee in San Francisco* (New York: 1848), 321, n. 30.
4. Cleland, op. cit., 264; Atherton, op. cit., 90–94; Phil Stong, *Gold in them Hills* (New York: 1957), passim.
5. Alexander Berry to Mrs. Shelley, 1 May 1850, Berry Pap., v. 25, Mit. Lib.
6. *S.M.H.*, 3 and 6 Oct. 1849.
7. Immigration Office, 13 May 1850, Col. Sec. Pap., 50/4839, Mit. Lib.
8. Tas. Arch., C.S.O. 24/6/144.
9. Ibid., Acc. No. 8/1462.
10. *S.M.H.*, 25 Feb. 1850.
11. Ibid.
12. *New Zealander*, 28 Nov. 1849.
13. *S.M.H.*, 29 Aug. 1849.
14. *S.M.H.*, 24, 25 and 26 Sep. and 3 Oct. 1849 and 9 and 11 Feb. 1850; H.R., Hon.; San Francisco arrivals as in n. 12, Chapter Ten.
15. *S.M.H.*, 25 Sep. 1849.
16. *S.M.H.*, 14 Sep. 1849.
17. *S.M.H.*, 15 Nov. 1849.
18. *S.M.H.*, 16 Nov. 1849, 3, 8 and 9 Apr. 1850.
19. *S.M.H.*, 2 Apr. 1850.
20. *S.M.H.*, 6 Apr. 1850. I have been unable to locate this petition.
21. *S.M.H.*, 26 Jan. 1850. For the difficulties over the *Harmony*, see ante, p. 100–1.
22. Johnson Dean, *A Trip to California in 1850–3, with Chapters on South Seas Islands, Port Phillip and Beautiful Tasmania* (Hobart: n.d.).
23. Ibid., 9.
24. Ibid., 10–12.
25. *S.M.H.*, 13 May 1850.
26. *S.M.H.*, 29 Dec. 1849.

27. Col. Sec. Pap., 50/245, Browne to Government Emigration Officer, 8 Jan. 1850, Mit. Lib.; *Government Gazette*, 11 Jan. 1850.
28. William Shaw, *Golden Dreams and Walking Realities, being the Adventures of a Gold Seeker in California and the Pacific Islands* (London : 1851).
29. Johnson Dean, op. cit., 17.
30. John Jamison to Elspeth Jamison, 11 Dec. 1849, *S.M.H.*, 4 Mar. 1850.
31. Thomas Hinigan to the Editors of the *S.M.H.*, 8 Mar. 1850, *S.M.H.*, 20 May 1850.
32. Ibid.
33. John Jamison to Elspeth Jamison, op. cit.
34. *S.M.H.*, 7 Feb. 1850.
35. Thomas Hinigan to the Editors of the *S.M.H.*, op. cit.
36. *S.M.H.*, 10 June 1850.
37. William Shaw, op. cit.
38. *S.M.H.*, 25 Mar. 1850.
39. Hobler Journal, Mit. Lib., v, vi.
40. Ibid., vi, 161–3.
41. Ibid., vi, 165, 171.
42. Ibid., vi, 172.
43. Ibid., vi, 193.
44. Ibid., 11 Sep. 1849.
45. Ibid., vii, 114.
46. Ibid., viii, 9 Mar. 1851.
47. A copy of this log is in the possession of Mrs. F. G. Marginson, of Hamilton, Brisbane, Queensland.
48. Fox to H. H. Nathan, 11 Aug. 1851, and to Alger, 13 Aug. 1851. Copies sent to the author by Mrs. Marginson.
49. Fox to Ellen Fox, 29 Dec. 1851; *S.M.H.*, 17 Dec. 1851; *Nautical Magazine*, May, 1856. Copies sent to the author by Mrs. Marginson.

CHAPTER 12

1. Ante, p. 105.
2. S.R., Arr., Mit. Lib., Jan. 1851, passim.
3. Ibid., *Emma*, 7 Jan. 1851; Eric W. Dunlop, *The Golden Fifties*, Jour. R.A.H.S., xxxvii, 23–4.
4. Dunlop, op. cit., discusses the circumstances of Hargraves's discovery.
5. Ibid., 39.

THESE APPENDIXES are compiled from various official shipping records and newspaper sources.

Honolulu arrival and sailing dates are from the Harbourmaster's Records, Hawaiian Archives, Honolulu.

The arrival dates at San Francisco, owing to the destruction by fire or earthquake of official records, have been taken from contemporary newspaper sources searched by Mr. Barr Thompkins, of the Bancroft Library, University of California, or Mrs. Hester Robinson, of the Society of California Pioneers.

New Zealand sailing dates were furnished by Mr. R. Duthie, City Librarian, Auckland Public Libraries. Passengers in vessels from Australia which touched at New Zealand do not include any who embarked at the New Zealand port; the figures are those who sailed from Australia only.

The totals of passengers on vessels sailing from Launceston have been taken from the George Town Police Record (Tas. Arch., Acc. 8/1462). Newcastle sailings, with one exception, are excluded.

Abbreviations: Bg =Brig; Bk =Barque; Bn =Brigantine or Barquentine; Cut =Cutter; K =Ketch; S =Ship; Sch =Schooner; * =American vessel. † =Number of cabin and steerage passengers not given separately.

Notes to the appendixes appear at the end of the appendixes.

APPENDIX 1: Sailings for California from Sydney, N.S.W., 1849–1850

Sailed 1849	Vessel	Rig	Ton	Built at	Year	Master	New Zealand		Honolulu		'Frisco		No of Passengers	
							Arrived	Sailed	Arrived	Sailed	Arrived	days	C.	S.
8 Jan	Plymouth	Sch	86		1838	Geo H Gould[1]			21 Mar	10 Apr	5 May	117	—	—
16 Jan	Despatch	Sch	139	Jersey	1847	Wm Francis Plant			28 Mar	31 Mar	25 Apr	99	1	—
20 Jan	William Hill	Bg	119	Clarence River	1839	J Macdonald					18 Apr	88	3	—
21 Jan	Eleanor Lancaster	Bk	438	Maryport		F W Lodge					2 Apr	71	52†	
21 Jan	Lindsays	Bk	219[a]			W Mackenzie					18 June	148	3	
31 Jan	Louisa	Bg	182	Southtown	1834	W N Millton			23 Apr	18 May	7 May	96	34†	
19 Feb	Inez	S	356	*		Wm L Jackson			14 Apr	17 Apr	4 May	74	18†	
4 Apr	Sabine	Bg	175	*		Geo W Town					1 July	88	24†	
14 Apr	Fanny	Bg	171	Chittagong	1838	Francis D Leathard	?	5 June			29 Aug	137	14†	
23 Apr	Spencer	Bg	222	Workington	1829	C Bell					6 Aug	105	14†	
24 May	Volunteer	Bk	250			W H Wingfield	2 June	13 June			[3]		54†	
26 May	Louisa	Bk	307	Calcutta	1824	Robt Mailler					29 Aug	95	78†	
5 June	Regia	Bg	181	Cochin	1835	Robt Johnson					29 Aug	85	32†	
28 June	Star of China	Sch	101	Manning River	1843	Howard Dowker	8 July	15 July			10 Nov	135	68†	
17 July	Elizabeth Archer	Bk	338	Maryport	1846	Chas Cobb					6 Oct	81	124†	
27 July	Spec	Bg	168	Cochin	1843	Geo Dicey	?	21 Aug			12 Nov	108	54†	
27 Aug	Margaret	Bg	186	Truro, NS	1837	Wm Browne McLeod	?	?	16 Nov	26 Nov	27 Dec	122	87†	
5 Sept	Giraffe	Bg	260	South Shields	1834	Ralph Robinson					2 Dec	88	4	—
6 Sep	Coquette	Sch	72	St Vincent, NSW	1840	Geo Elliott					27 Nov	82	3	—
12 Sep	Inchinnan	Bk	565	Sunderland	1844	Henry Pearse	?	26 Sep			2 Dec	81	219†	
23 Sep	Courier de Tahiti	S	387	Leith	1834	John Butler			19 Dec	16 Jan	13 Feb	143	14†	
25 Sep	Chearful	Bn	124	Sydney	1840	Edw Williams			15 Jan	19 Jan	20 Feb	148	86†	
28 Sep	Georgiana	Cut	25	Lake Macquarie	1845	Lawrence Johnson					13 Feb	138	1	
29 Sep	Ebenezer	Sch	90	Sunderland	1845	Joseph Hunter					13 Dec	75	13	
7 Oct	Chaseley	S	515	Holyhead	1835	C F Aldrich					5 Jan	90	13	11
12 Oct	Marian Watson	Sch	146	Yarmouth	1846	Evans					26 Feb	137	4	
12 Oct	Maria	Bk	460	Williams River	1849	Fred W Plank			17 Dec	22 Dec	15 Jan	95	193†	—
15 Oct	Enchantress	Bg	146	Newcastle	1828	Thos Spencer Boyes[4]					15 Jan	92	5	
15 Oct	Duke of Roxburgh	Bk	498	Quebec	1815	G P Collard					14 Jan	91	165†	—
23 Oct[5]	Fame	Bk	203			Joseph Bradley					19 Mar	147	15†	
23 Oct	Sarah Ann	Sch	184	Clarence River		John Russell					5 Feb	105	20†	
24 Oct	William Hill	Bg	119	*		Orr					30 Jan	98	15†	
25 Oct	Harrison	S	371	Pt Macquarie	1847	A D Sherman					8 Feb	106	15†	
29 Oct	Petrel	Sch	69	*	1844	Campbell[6]	?	20 Nov	9 Feb	27 Feb	28 Mar	150	15†	
27 Oct	Eliza	Sch	33			F J King					7 Apr	162	?	
30 Oct	Primus	K	38	Sydney	1845	Nicholas Lane			4 Jan	19 Jan	17 Feb	110	23†	
6 Nov	Gleaner	Sch	42	Manning River	1848	John Johnson					30 Mar	144	09†	
7 Nov	Lady Howden	Bg	210			C H Cl…					20 Feb	105		—

Dep.	Ship	Rig	Tons	From	Built	Master				Arrived	Days	No.	
14 Nov	Victoria	Bk	589	Nova Scotia	1848	John Carphin		21 Jan	26 Jan	18 Feb	96	272†	—
3 Dec	Hyndes	Cut	34	Sydney	1832	Edw Catlin				6 Apr	124	1	—
5 Dec	Bee	Bg	134	Mevagissey	1818	Addams				10 Apr	126	29	?
6 Dec	Sabine[7]	Bg	175	*		Geo Barmore						45†	—
12 Dec	Lord Hobart	Bg	161	Salcombe	1805	Geo Banks				24 Apr	133		
16 Dec	Salacia	Bg	296	Whitby	1827	R Armstrong				27 Apr	132	2	
17 Dec	Sea Gull	Sch	62	Ultimo, Sydney	1849	Rich H A Napper				1 Apr	105	21†	—
23 Dec	Seringapatam	S	398	Bombay	1799	F Lovett[8]				18 Mar	85	158†	
28 Dec	Gloucester	Bk	297		?	Tardiff	28 Jan			10 Mar	72	115†	
1850													
4 Jan	Rose	Sch	38	Hawkesbury	1849	Robt Lorne Pattison		24 Mar	29 Mar	30 Apr	116	4	
9 Jan	Deborah	Bg	121	Yarmouth	1841	Thos M Machattie	24 Feb			30 Apr	111	12†	
23 Jan	Hamlet	Bk	420	Sunderland	1841	Wilson				13 June	141	13†	
28 Jan	Orator	Bk	440	Clarence River	1849	Wm Tayt		30 Apr	4 May	?		168†	
29 Jan	Esther	Sch	54		1849	Patrick Cooney[9]	?			31 May	122	15†	
4 Feb	Reaper	Bk	423	Whitby		James Rose	18 Mar			5 June	121	46†	
7 Feb	Harmony	S	520		1809	John Smith Papps				2 July	145	217†	
10 Feb	Johanne & Oluffa	Sch	139			N L Enger				30 Apr	79	2	
17 Feb	Ralph Bernal	Bk	314	Sunderland	1835	G MacLaren	?			5 June	108	107	
27 Feb	William and Mary	Bk	506	Sunderland	1849	Peters				11 June	104	263†	—
6 Mar	Ellen	Bn	40	Sydney	1850	Patrick Cooney[9]				19 June	105	2	
12 Mar	Velocity	Bn	138	Wallace, NS	1840	Thos McVeigh		18 May	18 May	13 June	93	9†	
14 Mar	Balmoral	S	357	Peterhead	1848	G Pryde		26 Apr	14 May	2 June	80	26†	
14 Mar	Louisa[10]	Bg	182	Southtown	1834	W N Millton				10 June	88	2	
16 Mar	Johannes Sarkies	Bk	455	Sunderland		Wm Gillam				17 June	93	7	64
24 Mar	Oceanie	S	533	Sunderland		Gustavus Radou	26 Apr	7 June	10 Aug[11]	?19 July	110	27†	—
31 Mar	Raymond	Bk	498	Douglas, Isle of Man	1840	Hart				17 July	75	25†	—
3 Apr	Crishna	Bk	271	Cochin	1843	Spence	16 May			25 June	80	10†	
6 Apr	Spec	Bg	168		1843	Geo Dicey	28 May			17 Aug	132	1	
7 Apr	Le Baron	Bk	170			Chadwick				29 June	82	223†	
8 Apr	Una	S	793	Liverpool		Causzar				29 June	75	6†	
15 Apr	Swallow	Bk	243	Whitehaven		Seagrove				28 July	93	17†	
25 Apr	Laura	Bk	329	Jersey		Dembrill				8 Aug	95	25†	
5 May	Portenia	Bg	221		1829	Antonio L Milatovich		27 June	3 July	30 July	86	2	
5 May	Despatch	Sch	139		1829	Wm Francis Plant	?			?28 Aug	106	68†	
14 May	John Munn	Bk	638	Calcutta	1838	Pearson				13 Aug	90		
15 May	Flinders	Sch	15	Manning River		Cameron				20 Sep	120	17†	
23 May	Brightman	Bk	384	Sunderland	1826	Colin Geo Cowley		1 Aug	19 Aug	17 Aug	80	8†	—
29 May	Rosetta Joseph	Bk	265	Cochin	1847	Andrew Patrick	9 Aug			12 Oct	146	5†	
29 May	Sarah Scott	Bk	382		1839	T Spedding	?			22 Aug	85	5	
29 May	Regia	Bg	181	Sunderland	1835	Robert Johnson	?			19 Sep	111		
31 May	Braemar	Bk	360	Cochin		Titherington				11 Oct	123		—
10 June	Deucalion[12]	S	513	*		Green							—

Sailed 1849	Vessel	Rig	Ton	Built at	Year	Master	New Zealand Arrived	New Zealand Sailed	Honolulu Arrived	Honolulu Sailed	'Frisco Arrived	days	No of Passengers C.	S.
12 June	Smyrna	Bk	272	*	1837	Ankers					?21 Aug	70	2	—
9 July	Margaret	Bg	186	Truro, NS	1845	Wm Browne McLeod	?	?			28 Sep	81	—	—
29 July	Chaseley[13]	S	516	Sunderland		Brown					5 Jan	160	—	—
29 Aug	Eleanor Lancaster	Bk	438	Maryport	1839	F W Lodge			22 Oct	11 Nov	11 Dec	104	33†	—
29 Aug	Wigeon	Bg	280			J J Capes					14 Dec	107	12†	—
4 Sep	Arabian	Sch	113			Tucker					23 Nov	80	—	—
6 Sep	Louisa	Bk	307	Calcutta	1834	Robt Mailler					13 Nov	68	1	—
21 Sep	Ellis	Sch	134			Caleff					23 Dec	93	—	—
9 Oct	Maria	Bk	460	Yarmouth	1846	Fred W Plank					4 Jan	87	26†	—
16 Oct	Rosalind[14]	Bg	271			Elliott							4	—
17 Oct	Victoria	Bk	589	Nova Scotia	1848	John Carphin					7 Jan	82	10†	—
20 Oct	Balmoral	S	357	Peterhead	1848	Geo Pryde			30 Nov	13 Dec	30 Dec	71	20†	—
1 Nov	Samuel Churchman	Bg	221	*		Newall					26 Jan	86	4	—
5 Nov	Mary Adeline	Bg	184	*		Pearson					7 Feb	94	—	—
10 Nov	Eudora[15]	Bk	208	Chepstow	1835	John Gourlay			14 Jan	11 Feb			8†	—
11 Nov	Rhone[16]	S	471	*		A W Dennis							9†	—
6 Dec	York	S	433			Arthur					22 Feb	78	37†	—
7 Dec	Louisa Baillie	S	413	London	1834	Robt Roxby			12 Feb	26 Feb	24 Mar	107	23†	—
24 Dec	Giraffe	Bg	260	South Shields	1834	Ralph Robinson			4 Apr	14 Apr			3	—
31 Dec	Lanark	Bg	299	*		Woodberry					25 Mar	84	38†	—

APPENDIX 2: Sailings for California from Tasmania, 1849–1850

(Note: H before date of sailing=sailed from Hobart; L=from Launceston)

Sailed	Vessel	Rig	Ton	Built at	Year	Master	New Zealand Arrived	New Zealand Sailed	Honolulu Arrived	Honolulu Sailed	'Frisco Arrived	days	No of Passengers C.	S.
H 21 Jan	Eliza	Sch	118	Port Arthur	1843	Wm Daniel Chard			9 Apr	11 Apr	4 May	103	—	—
H 13 Feb	Osprey	Sch	148	Bristol	1834	Alfred Griggs			19 Apr	20 Apr	20 May	96	—	—
H 17 Feb	Martha & Elizabeth	Sch	81	Clarence River	1843	Wm Murray	?	?	24 June	13 July[17]			—	—
H 14 Apr	Lady Leigh	Sch	55	Newport	1835	B White			13 June	12 July	10 Aug	118	19†	—
H 6 June	Bandicoot	Sch	113	Hobart	1838	Philip Cannaway			10 Sep	17 Sep	?			
H 6 June	Harriet Nathan	Bk	113	Hobart	1844	John Archer					17 Sep	103	26†	—
H 23 June	Vansittart	Cut	79	Ipswich	1821	Gill					4 Nov	134	1	
H 27 June	John Bull	Bn	71	Mercury Bay, NZ	1845	T E Robinson	17 July	26 July			29 Oct	124	33†	
H 3 July	William Melville	Bk	219	Newport	1844	Geo Thomas					29 Sep	88	30†	
H 14 July	Munford	Sch	169	Southtown	1835	John Hayle					30 Oct	108	22†	
L 4 Aug	Spartan	Bk	380		1828	J B Pain					31 Oct	88	41†	
L 26 Aug	Duchess of Clarence	Bk	275	Ilfracombe		Cole					22 Nov	88	64†	

Date	Ship	Rig	Tons	Port	Year	Master			Arrival	Days	No.
H 11 Oct	Fair Tasmanian	Bk	155	Hobart	1848	Alex Ellis			29 Dec	79	
H 6 Dec	Caroline[18]	Bk	330	Chepstow	1835	Wm C Perry	28 Mar	2 Apr	7 May	148	52†
H 10 Dec	Eudora	Bk	208	Carleton, Canada	1834	John R Gourley			4 May	130	70†
H 25 Dec	Maquasha	Bg	151			Thomas Hannah					16†
1850											
H 1 Jan	Margaret Brock	Bk	245	Hobart	1848	MacMurken			27 Mar	85	10†
H 9 Jan	Dorset	Bg	82	Liverpool	1838	John Searle Bowden			30 April	111	10†
H 10 Jan	Eagle[19]	Sch	93	Harwich	1818	Winter					—
H 2 Feb	Elizabeth Starbuck	S	400			Parker					98†
H 5 Feb	Cacique	Bk	150	Isle of Man	1831	Mansfield	27 Apr	27 May	21 May	105	60†
H 20 Feb	Petrel[20]	Sch	195	River Tamar	1848	Wm Carder			11 Nov	?	9†
H 21 Feb	I Don't Know[21]	Sch	75	Bay of Islands	1843	Griffith					9†
H 22 Feb	Eliza	Sch	118	Port Arthur	1843	Wm Daniel Chard	22 May	3 June	22 May	89	12†
H 23 Feb	Palmyra	Bk	146			Lindsay			19 June	116	25†
L 26 Feb	Swan	Bg	149	Launceston	1844	Joseph Ayres			2 July	126	15†
H 27 Feb	Alert	Sch	92	Bellingen River	1846	James Taylor			17 June	110	1
H 28 Feb	Esperanza	Bg	141	Hobart	1847	Henry Tanner			14 June	106	19†
H 1 Mar	Pryde	Bg	204	Quebec	1842	Jas Wm Robinson	7 June	6 Aug	17 June	108	31†
H 2 Mar	Lady Leigh	Sch	118	Newport	1835	B White	12 Mar	19 Mar	1 July	107	30†
H 4 Mar	Sisters	Bg	130	Hobart	1840	Hugh Clark	19 Mar	31 Mar	8 July	119	17†
H 5 Mar	Triton	Bg	120	Bristol	1838	Wm Johnson	21 Mar	30 Mar	9 Sep	126	60†
H 12 Mar	Augusta	Bk	372	Sunderland	1846	Thos L Cooke			15 June	181	35†
L 20 Mar	Cape Horn	Bk	174	Greenock	1845	W F Saunders			15 June	87	3
H 22 Mar	Harriet Nathan	Bk	113	Hobart	1844	John Archer			25 June	85	19†
L 22 Mar	Halcyon	Bg	174			A T Wood			1 July	95	20†
H 23 Mar	Frances	Sch	123	Littlehampton	1835	Hill			1 July	100	50†
H 23 Mar	Timbo	Bk	216	Southtown	1826	Wm Marr	?		17 June	100	1
L 24 Mar	Tamar	Sch	119			Edwin Whiting			28 July	85	36†
L 30 Mar	William Melville	Bk	219	Newport	1844	Geo Thomas			1 July	120	18†
H 5 Apr	Henry Harbeck	Bk	491			Merwin			11 July	87	?
H 6 Apr	John & Charlotte	Sch	93	Manning River	1840	John Lovitt			?	86	5†
H 12 Apr	Auriga	Bk	232	London	1825	Harris			10 Aug	90	11†
H 20 Apr	Favorite	Sch	250						25 Aug	111	33†
L 21 Apr	Union[22]	Bg	166	Huon River	1849	Arnold Grainger			5 Aug	108	25†
L 9 May	Jane Frances	Bk	391			J Brown			3 Aug	87	4†
H 10 May	Ralph Thomson	Bk	385	Newcastle	1847	Atkinson			2 Sep	85	64†
L 11 May	Lawsons	Bg				Robt Ewart			19 Sep	113	14†
L 12 May	Spartan	Bk	380			J B Pain			9 Sep	107	6†
L 4 June	Xylon	S				Edw McKenzie			20 Oct	82	59†
H 19 June	Panama	Bk	313	Hobart	1850	Davidson			10 Oct	96	?
H 16 July	Rebecca	Bk	343	Greenock	1816	Murray			29 Nov	84	?
H 18 July	Amity Hall[23]	Bk	420	Sunderland	1831	Johnson				93	
H 27 July	Fair Tasmanian[24]	Bk	155	Hobart	1848	Alex Ellis					

159

Sailed	Vessel	Rig	Ton	Built at	Year	Master	NZ Arrived	NZ Sailed	Honolulu Arrived	Honolulu Sailed	'Frisco Arrived	days	Pass. C.	Pass. S.
1850														
H 9 Oct	Baretto Junior	Bk	523	Calcutta	1818	Iven Huggins					27 Dec	79		5†
H 22 Oct	Duchess of Clarence	Bk	275	Ilfracombe	1828	Henry G Cole			26 Dec	11 Jan	8 Feb	109		?
L 16 Nov	Rory O'More					James Brennan					2 Feb	78		4†

APPENDIX 3: Sailings for California from Adelaide, 1849–1850

Sailed	Vessel	Rig	Ton	Built at	Year	Master	NZ Arrived	NZ Sailed	Honolulu Arrived	Honolulu Sailed	'Frisco Arrived	days	Pass. C.	Pass. S.
1849														
3 Mar	Sophia Margaret	Sch	98	Deptford, NSW	1846	Wm Barrett	24 June	1 July			18 June	107		29†
8 June	Mazeppa	S	163			John Mordaunt	?	4 Aug			14 Oct	128		19†
14 July	Joseph Albino	Sch	142			Thos Allen					26 Oct	104		44†
1850														
12 Jan	Pauline	Bk	441	Harrington	1835	L Stelljes					5 Apr	83		165†
17 Jan	Colonist	Bk	261			Marshall	?	15 Mar			27 May	130		113†
16 Feb	Robert Henderson	Bk	368	Sunderland	1844	Toohig					23 June	127		176†
21 Mar	Agincourt[25]	S	669			Cumberland					30 July	131		134†
3 Apr	Broadaxe[26]	Bg				Lamb					1 Aug	120		?
19 Apr	Henrietta[27]	Sch	104			Waugh					8 Aug	111		—
27 May	Emma Sherratt	Bg				Cock					9 Sep	105		?

APPENDIX 4: Sailings for California from Melbourne, 1849–1850

Sailed	Vessel	Rig	Ton	Built at	Year	Master	NZ Arrived	NZ Sailed	Honolulu Arrived	Honolulu Sailed	'Frisco Arrived	days	Pass. C.	Pass. S.
1849														
27 June	William Watson	Bk	480	Dumbarton	1845	E Morrison					17 Sep	82	25	136
15 July	Union	Sch	74	D'Entrecasteaux Channel	1848	E T Barnes					4 Oct	81	15	25
1850														
6 Jan	River Chief	Bg	159	Peterhead	1848	Wm E Matthews	?	31 Jan	7 May	29 May	2 July	177		?
25 Jan	Lalla Rookh	Bg	156			H Milner	10 Mar	15 Mar			23 May	118		?
2 Apr	Raven	Bg	170			Brown					1 July	90		?

APPENDIX 3: Sailings for California from New Zealand, 1849–1850

(Note: Does not include all vessels which called en route from Australia. A before date of sailing=sailed from Auckland; W=from Wellington)

Date sailed	Vessel	Rig	Tons	Built	Year	Master			Arrived	Days	Passengers	
1849												
A 13 Mar	Deborah	Sch	121	Kaipara, NZ		Andrew Bliss			21 June	100	18†	
A 17 June	Clyde	Sch	40		1849	Alex McLean	6 Sep		23 Oct	128	25†	
A 4 Aug	Ennerdale	Bk	450			J G Balliston			21 Oct	78	25†	
A 20 Aug	Frederick	Sch	73	Macleay River	1848	Hunt	10 Sep		10 Dec	112	11†	
A 10 Sep	Thomas Lord	Sch	70	Sydney	1842	Henry Cain			28 Dec	109	12†	
A 20 Oct	Marys	Sch	62	Kangaroo Pt, Tas	1840	Granger	15 Nov		19 Feb	122	9†	
A 2 Nov	Elizabeth[28]	Sch	21	Auckland	1849	Wm Talbot		27 Nov	10 Feb	100	—	—
A 13 Nov	Maukin	Bg	106	Auckland	1846	Bowden			3 Feb	82	1	—
A 18 Nov	Pilgrim	Bk	347	Liverpool	1839	Joseph Frances			4 Feb	78	45†	
A 4 Dec	Pembroke	Bk	200			E S Porter			2 Apr	119	7†	
A 4 Dec	Wanderer	Yacht	84	Isle of Wight		Benjamin Boyd	26 Feb	11 Mar	29 Mar	115	?	—
A 5 Dec	Kiwi	Bg	87	Kaipara	1849	McLean			23 Mar	108	8†	
A 23 Dec	Joseph Cripps	Sch	78	Circular Head	1840	McFarlane			1 Apr	99	1	
A 25 Dec	Vulcan	Sch	47	Auckland	1849	Teviotdale			22 Sep	271	35†	
A 31 Dec	Eagle	Sch	23	Auckland	1849	Wm Aldwell			1 July	182	16†	
1850												
A 8 Jan	Avon	Bk	264	Whitby	1826	Alfred Silver	5 Mar		8 Apr	90	60†	
A 14 Jan	Enterprise[29]	Bg	253		1838	E Lovering	7 May	15 Apr			13†	
A 21 Jan	Fanny[30]	Bg	171	Chittagong	1838	Wm Twohey	30 Apr	10 June			9†	
A 5 Feb	Shamrock[31]	Sch	80		1831	W P Gray		14 May			3†	
A 10 Feb	Noble	Bk	252	Maine, USA		Parker			24 June	134	7†	
A 20 Feb	Saltillo[32]	Bk	162			Smith			27 Apr	66	—	—
A 27 Feb	Josephine	Bk	310			Smith			7 June	100	5†	
A 6 Feb	Salacia	Bk	296	Whitby	1827	Armstrong			27 Apr	80	?	
A 11 Mar	Sir John Franklin	Sch	52	Port Arthur	1838	J Church			15 June	96	2	
A 14 Mar	William & James	Sch	75	Brisbane Water	1849	Wm Currey			17 June	95	7†	
W 19 Mar	Thames	Bk	407	London	1827	Hadley			30 Apr	42	—	—
A 23 Mar	Two Friends	Bg	207			Courtenay			22 June	91	3†	
A 23 Mar	Johnstone	S	436	Liverpool	1832	T B Harrison			3 June	72	16	
A 2 Apr	Commodore	S	489	Dumbarton	1843	James Broadfoot			27 June	86	26†	
A 6 Apr	Post Boy	Sch	31	Mahurangi	1849	Parker			2 July	87	5†	
W 25 Apr	Minerva	Bg	110	Cowes	1812	Thos Birkenshaw			12 Sep	140	?	
W 19 May	Artemisia	Bk	558	Sunderland	1847	John P Ridley			5 Aug	78	12†	
A 4 June	Constant[33]	S	535	Hylton	1843	Combes					12†	70
A 16 July	Inchinnan	Bk	565	Sunderland	1844	Henry Pearse			29 Sep	75	12†	
A 19 July	Lord Stanley	Bk	400			Hugh McKay			18 Oct	91	15†	
W 25 Aug	Orion	S	534			Ray			1 Nov	68	?	
W 25 Aug	Harlequin	Sch	62	Sydney	1828	Price			25 Nov	92	?	
W 11 Sep	Return	Sch	76	Wellington	1849	Warren			14 Dec	94	?	

NOTES TO APPENDIXES

1. Replaced at Honolulu after vessel's sale by J.F. Church.
2. Condemned as a prize at the Vice Court of Admiralty, Bermuda, 15 Jan. 1833.
3. Reported to have arrived at Monterey, where her crew deserted her. I have been unable to trace her further history.
4. His surname may have been spelt Bayes.
5. Called at Newcastle, N.S.W., from where she probably sailed on 4 Nov. 1849.
6. On arrival at both Honolulu and San Francisco, her master was recorded as William Turnbull.
7. Totally lost at Upolu, 26 Jan. 1850.
8. His surname may have been Lovell, as given in Lloyd's Register and in arrival notice.
9. Captain Cooney's wife died a few days before the *Esther* sailed and although his name is recorded both in clearance and sailing notices, it seems he did not sail until 6 Mar. 1850, when he left in command of the *Ellen*. On arrival at San Francisco the master of the *Esther* was recorded as Long.
10. There is a doubt whether this vessel arrived at San Francisco on 10 June, as the *Louisa* recorded at that date as arriving from Sydney is described as a brig of 290 tons commanded by Heslop. However, I have been unable to trace any *Louisa* answering this description as having left Sydney.
11. In the Harbourmaster's Records, Honolulu, she is recorded as sailing for Manila. There is a doubt whether she was destined for San Francisco when she left Sydney, and probably it was intended she should not go beyond Honolulu.
12. She called at Hobart and sailed from there on 24 July with eight passengers.
13. Sailed from Newcastle, N.S.W., but apparently called at Hobart and finally sailed from there. On arrival at San Francisco was reported as 93 days out from Hobart.
14. When 300 miles from land she developed a leak and put back, returning to port on 20 Oct. As her cargo was transferred to another vessel and she was hove down, she presumably did not resume her voyage.
15. Cleared for and sailed for San Francisco, but

apparently did not go beyond Honolulu. Harbourmaster's Records say that when she sailed from there
her destination was Newcastle, N.S.W.

16. Returned to port leaky on 21 Nov. and subsequently
was sold. Did not resume her voyage in 1850.

17. Did not reach San Francisco, although that was her
destination when she left Hobart. On sailing from
Honolulu her destination was given as Hong Kong.
(Harbourmaster's Records.)

18. Totally wrecked off Honolulu Heads, 26 Mar. 1850.

19. Wrecked Bay of Islands, N.Z. Her master's name is
also given as Gray.

20. When she left Honolulu on 27 May her destination
was given as Hobart, but her return to Hobart and
subsequent departure for San Francisco have not
been traced. She may have gone elsewhere and then
on to San Francisco.

21. Went missing on this passage.

22. The record of the Police Office, George Town (Tas
Arch. Acc. No. 8/1462) states she returned on
27 Apr., but gives no subsequent sailing date.

23. Date of sailing not recorded, but would have been
18 July if record of arrival is correct.

24. Date of sailing not recorded, but if information given
at time of her arrival at San Francisco is correct, it
would have been 27 July.

25. Called at Hobart and sailed from there on 21 Apr.
1850.

26. Departure not recorded, but information given at
time of arrival at San Francisco indicates she would
have sailed originally on 3 Apr. 1850.

27. Called at Sydney, from where she sailed on 19 or
20 May 1850.

28. Wrongly reported wrecked en route to California.

29. Cleared and sailed from Auckland for San Francisco,
but when she sailed from Honolulu, Harbourmaster's Records state she was bound for Tahiti. No
record of her arrival at San Francisco has been
found.

30. Cleared and sailed for San Francisco, but Harbourmaster's Records, Honolulu, indicate that when she
sailed from there her destination was Auckland. No
record of her arrival at San Francisco has been
found.

31. Cleared and sailed for San Francisco from Auckland, but when she sailed from Honolulu, Harbourmaster's Records give her destination as Auckland. No record of her arrival at San Francisco has been found.
32. Actually sailed from Monganui.
33. Sailed and cleared for San Francisco, but no record of her arrival there has been found.

166